a kids' guide to
HAMILTON
the musical

written by
Amanda Bjerkan Hennessy

illustrated by
Isabella Bjerkan

Special thanks to Scott, my rock, and all my family and friends who encouraged me along this journey.

This is a work of creative nonfiction. It shares the stories of real people and real events. It also explains the dramatization of these events as told in the musical "Hamilton." It is an unofficial guide and is not authorized by the show's creator, publisher, or producer.

Original illustrations by Isabella Bjerkan
Cover art design by Erin Relyea Flores

A Kids' Guide to Hamilton the Musical is printed by Kindle Direct Publishing with chlorine-free ink on FSC certified, acid-free paper made from 30% post-consumer waste recycled material.

ISBN: 9798668353873
Independently published

www.akidsguidetohamilton.com

FIRST EDITION   3 4 5 6 7 8 9 10

For Giselle and Nathan. Thank you for inspiring this book and for amazing me each and every day with your curiosity, creativity, and compassion.

preface

A message to you, the reader:

I'm SUPER excited you got this book about the incredible musical, "Hamilton." Maybe you're a huge fan of the songs, or maybe you've never heard any of them before. Either way, this book is for you!

My kids (who are six and eight years old) love the music from the show, but for a long time they didn't really understand what was happening in the story. I explained the songs when they asked me questions, and that helped. I decided to write this book to help other kids who might have questions, too—like you!

Did you know that **every song** in "Hamilton" was written by a man named Lin-Manuel Miranda? He had help on some of the songs, but he wrote most of them all by himself. That's pretty amazing, especially since there are **46 songs**! (Fun fact: Lin also wrote most of the songs for the Disney animated film, "Moana"!)

Lin was inspired by a book he read about Alexander Hamilton, which was written by a man named Ron Chernow. When Lin turned Alexander's fascinating life into a musical, he **changed some parts** of the real story a little bit. Sometimes he changed it to make the story more interesting, and sometimes he changed it to make it easier to understand. In this book, you'll see notes at the end of most chapters that tell you what **really** happened.

I hope learning about the stories in the songs from "Hamilton" helps you love and appreciate them even more.

Happy reading!

- Amanda

introduction:
how to use this book

- Each chapter is about one song from the show.
- There are three different features in the book to help you learn more:

Musical Notes explain different styles of music in the songs. Sometimes they explain what the music means.

> ♪ **Musical Note:** The music and words, or lyrics, to the song Philip and Eliza sing are the same as the duel countdown music from "Ten Duel Commandments."

Sidebars explain words or ideas you might not know. These words and more are also in the Glossary at the back of the book.

> **Legacy:** This word comes up a lot in "Hamilton." It basically means what people remember about you after you are gone.

Footnotes at the end of a chapter give extra details about what actually happened in real life.

You will see a small **1** in the story that shows you what the first footnote is about. Each footnote is explained at the end of the chapter it is in.

who's who

SAMUEL SEABURY
Loyal to King George

KING GEORGE III
Ruler of
Great Britain

GEORGE WASHINGTON
Commander-in-Chief of
Continental Army,
First U.S. President

AARON BURR
Alexander's
friend-then-enemy

ALEXANDER HAMILTON
Star of this story, a
"founding father" of
the United States

HERCULES MULLIGAN
Alexander's friend, a
tailor-turned-spy

MARQUIS DE LAFAYETTE
Alexander's friend
from France, a
military hero

JOHN LAURENS
Alexander's dear
friend, who tries
to end slavery

contents

ACT TWO

a kids' guide to
HAMILTON
the musical

— act one —

I. ALEXANDER HAMILTON
The first 18 years

This is the story of Alexander Hamilton, and how he overcame incredibly difficult challenges in his life to achieve many amazing things. What challenges did he face? How did he get through them? How did he grow up to become a "**founding father**" of the United States—one of just a few people who are most remembered for helping to create the country at the very beginning of its history? Alexander's story is a powerful example of how hard work, determination, and standing up for what you believe in can make a big difference in the world.[1]

Alexander grew up in the West Indies, on an island in the Caribbean Sea between Florida and South America. He was an **orphan**, which means he didn't have any parents in his life. His father was gone, and his mother got really sick and, sadly, died when Alexander was only about 12 years old.[2]

As a kid, Alexander read a LOT, worked very hard, and wanted *really* badly to be part of something important.

When he was 17,[3] a **hurricane**, which is a huge, powerful storm with lots of wind and rain, caused a lot of damage to Alexander's hometown. He knew he needed to do something big to get himself out of the horrible situation he was in. He wrote a very

Founding fathers: These are the few people in United States history who are thought of as doing the most work to create, or found, the country.

The founding fathers were: John Adams, Benjamin Franklin, Alexander Hamilton, John Jay, Thomas Jefferson, James Madison, and George Washington.

Each of these men did at least one of these things:

- helped the colonies join together
- wrote: the United States Declaration of Independence, the beginnings of the U.S. Constitution, the Federalist Papers supporting the new Constitution, the Treaty of Paris that ended the Revolutionary war
- led the Continental Army
- had very important jobs in the first years of the country

2

descriptive letter about the devastation, and it was **published**, or printed, in the newspaper.

Because he worked hard, because he kept going even when things got really challenging and scary, and because he held onto his dreams of creating a great life for himself, the letter Alexander wrote touched the hearts of people who read it.

Lots of people who read his letter were so moved by his story that they collected enough money to send him to the British **colonies** in North America, where he could get a great education. This gave him hope that he might have a better future.

Colonies: A colony is a group of people who live in a different place than the country they are originally from, but they are still part of their original country. The place where they live is also called a colony. The people are called **colonists**.

There were a few different countries that had colonies in North America, where the United States is. One of the countries was Great Britain. Their 13 colonies later became the beginning of the United States.

A lot of times, the British made deals, called **treaties**, with the Native Americans who lived on the land first, in order to get the land for themselves. Sometimes, there was war and fighting for the land.

Making colonies was a way for a country to get more goods, which are things that people grow or make and then sell. It also gave people who moved there a chance to start a new life and be part of a new community. And that was very exciting to a lot of people.

Alexander sailed away on a ship and arrived in New York, one of the British colonies. For a long time, New York has been known as a place where people from anywhere in the world can come and make a great life for themselves if they work hard. It's a place where someone can turn themselves into a whole new person and make their dreams of a better life come true. And that is exactly what Alexander wanted to do.

Looking back at Alexander's whole life, it is clear he always worked hard—he never liked to rest or take a break. He argued with people to defend what he believed in, he became a trusted friend of George Washington (who later became the first president of the United States), and he fell in love and had a family.

One thing a lot of big kids and grown-ups in the United States today know about Alexander Hamilton is that his life ended in a **duel**, or fight, with a man named Aaron Burr. Wonder why? Want to learn more about Alexander and all of the work he did to help create the United States of America over two hundred years ago? Keep reading to see how his story goes!

---

1 This song is an introduction. It gives an overview of Alexander's entire life, from his childhood to his death. It tells a little bit about who he was and what he did,

as sort of a sneak peek into the stories coming up in the rest of the songs.

2 We don't know for sure if Alexander was born in 1755 or 1757, but most people today who study history believe he was probably born in 1755 and decided to change his birth year when he moved to the colonies. He might have done that to make himself seem younger when he started college. When his mother died, he was either 11 or 13, depending on when he was really born.

3 The hurricane happened in 1772, so Alexander was either 15 or 17.

2. AARON BURR, SIR
Alexander and Aaron meet[1]

Alexander is in New York, and he is trying to find Aaron Burr, the man he will end up dueling many years later (but of course he doesn't know that yet!).

Alexander finds Aaron and tells him he wants to finish college quickly, just like Aaron did, and join the **revolution**.

He asks Aaron how he was able to graduate so fast, and Aaron says it was what his parents wished for and wanted most before they died. Alexander feels an immediate connection to Aaron, who is an **orphan** just like he is. Alexander is looking for a place where he can belong, so he's excited to find someone who might become his friend.

> **Revolution:** A war—a really big fight—started between Great Britain and its 13 colonies in North America in 1775. The colonists wanted to be their own country instead of having the King be in charge of them. So they fought in a *revolution* to change the government. This is called the American Revolutionary War, and it's a really big part of this whole story.

Alexander says he wishes there was a war.[2] **Why would he wish for a war?** During this time, being part of a war would give him a chance to prove he matters, create a better life for himself, and make a difference in the world. If he does a good job fighting in the war, he might get to be part of a higher **social class**. That means he might become more important, have more money, and have people remember him for a long time—all things he wants for his life.

Aaron thinks about things a little bit differently than Alexander does. He offers Alexander advice and tells him not to talk so much, and to smile more instead. He warns Alexander not to let people know what matters to him.

Social Class and Social Status: In Colonial America, just like many places around the world throughout history, a person was considered to belong to one of a few different social "classes," or groups. It's kind of a way to divide people up and give them a label based on how much money, education, or land they had, or what their job was.

A person in a higher class had more privileges, or special things they could do, than someone in a lower class. Most of the time, a person's social class depended on the family they were born into and never really changed. People usually spent most of their time with other people who were in the same social class.

Being in a higher class didn't make a person better than other people. It just meant they got to do more things because of the money they had and the people they knew. It doesn't really seem fair, but that's how it was and how it still is in a lot of places today.

Aaron thinks if you don't tell people what you believe in, then everyone will like you *and* you won't get in trouble or get hurt. Alexander thinks it's important to say what you believe and to speak up when something isn't the way you think it should be. **Who do you agree with, Aaron or Alexander? Why? Are there any times where you might agree with the other person's way of thinking?**

Aaron and Alexander walk together to go get a drink. When they arrive, three guys are already there, laughing and having fun: John Laurens, the Marquis de Lafayette, and Hercules Mulligan.[3] Alexander quickly becomes friends with all of them. They have a lot of the same beliefs as he does, and they all want to be a part of the war.

As they're talking about the revolution, Aaron says if they all want to speak out about what they believe, that's up to them. But he says he is going to stay quiet and keep his thoughts to himself instead. He doesn't want other people to not like him if they don't agree with what he thinks.[4]

Alexander asks Aaron, "If you don't stand up for anything, what will you fall for?" Alexander could mean a few different things. He could mean that Aaron might "fall" for anything, which means being tricked by people to believe things that aren't true or aren't good, if he doesn't stand up for what he believes. Or he could be asking Aaron, "What *are* you willing to 'fall' on the ground, or risk your life, for, Aaron?"

Alexander's new friends are very impressed with the way he talks, and they like that he speaks up about what he thinks is right. They are excited to have found a new friend who isn't afraid to tell people what he thinks.

---

1 This first meeting between Aaron and Alexander didn't happen in real life, but putting them together in the story this way shows us how different they are from each other. They probably really met sometime during the war.

2 The war had actually already started, a year before

this imaginary conversation, in 1775. A lot of events in this song are smooshed together a bit to make it easier to follow along with the story.

3 John Laurens became one of Alexander's closest friends. He was part of George Washington's military "family" with Alexander, fought bravely in the war, and worked really hard to try to end **slavery**. *(See Song #3 for an explanation of slavery.)*

Lafayette's full name was Marie-Joseph Paul Yves Roch Gilbert du Motier, Marquis de La Fayette (wow!). He left France to help the colonies fight for their freedom from Britain. "Marquis" was a title for a nobleman, someone who is almost like royalty.

Hercules Mulligan was born in Ireland and became a hero of the revolution by spying on British soldiers who came to his **tailor** shop, where he made and fixed clothes for people. He was part of the Sons of Liberty, a secret group that protected the rights of the colonists. He was one of Alexander's very first friends in America and helped him decide to support the colonies instead of Britain. Hercules probably never really met John or Lafayette in real life.

4 Aaron was not actually shy about supporting the colonies in the fight with Britain. He started fighting in the war right away, even before any of these other guys did.

3. MY SHOT
Alexander is not afraid to take risks

Alexander is proud of how smart and feisty he is, and he is not shy about telling people he's going to do lots of great things someday. He knows he might be too honest sometimes, but he wants people to hear what he has to say. Since he didn't grow up in the colonies or have a famous family, it is harder for him to get people's attention than it would be for someone most people already know.

He's working hard to survive, and he wants to **make a name** for himself, which means he wants people to know who he is and remember him when he's gone. He wants to have a better life than the one he started with, a life where he can afford the things he needs and wants.

Alexander tells his friends over and over again that he is not going to throw away his "**shot**," which means his chance, or opportunity. He will take any chance he gets to join the revolution, so he can hopefully do something great and get rewarded for it, too.

Alexander says one reason the colonies should fight for their freedom is because it's not fair for King George to take money from them and then spend it on stuff in Britain, the country where he lives. It's also not fair that he doesn't let them vote or make their own decisions.

Alexander's friends all have different reasons why the revolution is important to them. Alexander wants to fight for what's right and to get a better life. Lafayette believes kings and queens should not be in charge. Hercules, like Alexander, wants to make a better life for himself.[1] John wants to lead a group of **enslaved people,** or **slaves,** in the war to help them earn their freedom.

Aaron Burr keeps telling them if they speak out about

Enslaved: Enslaved people were forced to work without being paid. They were captured and then sold or traded to other people for goods, like food, cloth, drinks, and weapons. They were separated from their family and friends and taken to far-away places, like the American colonies. Most of the slaves in the colonies were taken from the continent of Africa.

Enslaved people were called **slaves.** They did not have any freedom and were not allowed to leave. Most enslaved people were forced to work their entire lives. Most of them worked in fields where crops were grown, but slave owners, or **enslavers,** forced them to do lots of different things, including chores inside the home.

Some enslaved people escaped by running away to places or states where slavery was not allowed. But that was very dangerous and hard to do. If they got caught, their enslavers would punish them badly.

When the Civil War ended in 1865, almost 100 years after the Revolutionary War against Britain, slavery finally became illegal everywhere in the United States.

their beliefs, they're going to get in big trouble with Great Britain or with other people who don't agree with them. Alexander tells Aaron again that he and his new friends don't care about that—they are all going to stand up and fight for what they believe is right. Alexander is very excited to finally have a group of friends, and he loves that they all care about the revolution as much as he does!

---

1 Hercules was actually already well-known and respected as a **tailor**, which is someone who sews and fixes clothes to fit individual customers. In "Hamilton," he is a bit louder and wilder than he was in real life.

4. THE STORY OF TONIGHT
Actions can change the world

Alexander and his friends know they might not still be alive when the war is over, but it's really important to them to be a part of it. They believe what they do now—fighting for freedom—will create something that lasts a long, long time. It will be something their children and lots of people who are born many years later will be really proud of and grateful for.

5. THE SCHUYLER SISTERS
Life is pretty exciting in New York City

Aaron Burr is walking in a busy part of the city. He says rich people, which are people with a lot of money, like to come into the city to see all the not-rich people working hard. They also think it's fun to be so close to the excitement of everyone who is talking about the war.

The three Schulyer sisters[1]—Angelica, Eliza, and Peggy—are best friends and visit the city to watch the men who are working. The sisters all have different feelings about the war and the activity in the streets, and we learn that Angelica is looking for someone with a smart brain. Aaron tries to **flirt** with her, or get her to like him. He hopes he might be able to convince her to marry him, but she is not impressed. She knows he doesn't really care about her and only wants to talk to her because her family has a lot of money.

Angelica reads a lot, is interested in **politics**, and speaks up for what she believes in—like equal rights for women. She quotes the Declaration of Independence and says, *"We hold these*

Politics: How a government works, especially the conversations and different ideas people have and the way decisions get made, is called politics.

truths to be self-evident, that all men are created equal." And she adds that when she meets Thomas Jefferson, she is going to make him change it to say all men *and women* are equal to one another.[2]

Eliza is thrilled to be in the big city. She looks around, marveling at everything happening around them, and she exclaims that they are all so lucky to be living near such an amazing place during this very exciting time. The three sisters point out how incredible it is that history is being made right now. They know how lucky they are to see it happening right in front of them.

1 Angelica, Eliza, and Peggy had two more sisters and three brothers, but they are not in this story.

2 The **Declaration of Independence** is the document Thomas Jefferson wrote for the colonies that told the king they wanted to finally be free from Britain.

6. FARMER REFUTED

Not everyone agrees with Alexander and his friends

Samuel Seabury is a **Loyalist**, which is someone who lives in the colonies and is loyal to the King and Great Britain. Samuel writes a few short, strongly-worded **pamphlets**, or papers, to try to convince people that the revolution is a bad idea.

Samuel doesn't think **Congress** is making the best choices for the colonies, and he thinks the King is pretty great. He thinks it's wrong for people to be fighting against the King, and he doesn't like that there is violence and a war going on.

Alexander hears Samuel reading his pamphlets and does not agree with them at all, so he gives a sassy response.[1] Alexander always stands up for what he believes in, and he's not afraid of what other people might think when he does.

> **Congress:** Congress is a part of how the United States government works. The people in each state vote to choose who they want to be in Congress to represent them. Members of Congress have discussions, and they create and vote on laws for the country. Any new law has to be passed, or approved, by Congress before the president can sign it and make it an official law.
>
> (continued)

18

(continued)

Before and during the war with Great Britain, the Continental Congress was in charge of talking with the King, helping with the war, and making some laws.

A few years after the war was over, the United States **Constitution** was written and became the new laws for the country. When that happened, the Continental Congress was replaced with Congress, which works pretty much the same way today as it did then. (See Song #29 for more about Congress.)

Alexander repeats some of Samuel's words and then **refutes** them, which means he argues against them and proves them wrong. It's his way of trying to show that his ideas—that the colonies should be in charge of themselves—are the *right* ones. **What do you think? Should the colonies let Britain be in charge of them, or should they try to become their own country in charge of themselves?**

---

1 Alexander and Samuel actually argued back and forth through the pamphlets they wrote, not by talking with each other in front of everyone.

7. YOU'LL BE BACK

A not-so-nice "love letter" from the King to the colonies

♪ **Musical Note**: If you listen to the music, you might notice that King George's music sounds different from most of the other songs from "Hamilton."

Most of the music in "Hamilton" is a few different types of music: rap, hip-hop, or R+B. But King George's songs are what is called British Invasion **pop music**. It is a style of music a lot of British bands in the 1960s used, like The Beatles. It feels like music from a long time ago, like the "old way" of music. King George also uses very simple rhymes. All of these differences in his music help us think of King George as "the old way" of doing things, and Alexander and his friends as "the new way," or more modern way.

King George III—the three "I"s mean "the third"—lives all the way across the Atlantic Ocean in Great Britain, far away from the colonies. The colonists are upset about being **taxed**[1], which means having to pay some of their money to the government, when they don't get to help decide what happens with that money.

King George talks about the colonies sort of as if they are his girlfriend who suddenly decides she doesn't like him anymore. He reminds the colonists about the agreement they made when they moved to America. He believes they should stay loyal to him by doing whatever he says, since he protected them during earlier wars. (Of course a girlfriend doesn't have to stay loyal to her boyfriend just because he helped protect her, but the King is being kind of crazy.) He is very unhappy that the colonies don't want to be with him anymore. He just wants things to go back to how they were in the beginning, when they didn't fight and it was easy for him to be in charge.

King George says some not-so-nice things to scare the colonists, like that he is going to send a huge army of battle ships to remind them how much he loves them. It's really his way of saying he's asking nicely for them to stop fighting with him, but if they don't listen, he will just force them to obey him. Yikes! He believes if the colonies really think about it, they will realize they need him and decide to stay with him.

King George is *sure* that if the colonies really want to have a war, Britain will win. In his mind, there is no way the colonies could ever beat the very powerful British army and navy. He says he'll go crazy without the colonies in his life .[2] He makes a few more threats about how he will hurt the colonies if they don't just do what he wants, and then he starts singing his silly, happy "da da da" tune again.

---

1 There were actually not a lot of taxes the colonists had to pay at this time. This was more of an excuse for them to complain about how the king and Britain didn't seem to really care about them very much. It made them want to be free from Britain and be in charge of themselves even more.

The colonists decided to show how upset they were during what is called the Boston Tea Party, where they took all the tea the king had sent from Britain—that they were going to have to pay taxes on—and dumped it into the ocean to ruin it. Well, that made the king **very** mad. He and the British Parliament (which was kind of like Congress, but for Britain) decided to make a bunch of laws to punish the colonists for trying to stand up against them.

2 King George really did become a bit crazy, or "mad," after the colonies won the war and their freedom from Britain.

8. RIGHT HAND MAN
George Washington needs help

The **battle** in Brooklyn[1], New York, is the biggest battle, or fight, during the Revolutionary War, and it's happening right now. General Howe is the leader of 32,000 British **troops**, or soldiers, that just arrived in New York on ships. They are ready to fight in the battle against the colonies.

George Washington is in charge of the **Continental Army**, which is what the colonial or American army was called. For him, being someone who lots of people admire and look up to is nice, but it's still pretty intimidating to be fighting against such a powerful army. On top of that, his soldiers keep leaving the war because it's really difficult and scary, which makes it even harder to lead the people who do stay.

When the British win the battle at Brooklyn and take control of the city, George knows he has to be extra smart to save his army and not lose the whole war. He doesn't have as many troops as the British do, and the British soldiers are better than the American soldiers, because they've had a lot more **training**, or practice. So he orders his troops to **retreat**, or turn away and leave, overnight. This way they will be able to get away while the British soldiers are asleep.[2]

The battles keep going on and on, and Hamilton and the

soldiers who fight with him do everything they can to make it harder for the British to win. They even steal some of their cannons![3]

It's incredibly hard to be in charge of so many soldiers in so many places, with so much craziness going on, so George asks for help. Aaron wants to help, but George doesn't really trust him. He sends Aaron away so he can talk to Alexander. He knows Alexander and Hercules stole cannons from the British, which was smart and brave. George also knows that some important people asked Alexander to write their letters for them, and he wonders why Alexander did not say "Yes."

George knows Alexander wants to fight in the war. He explains that it is an honor—and more challenging—to do the behind-the-scenes work that is so critical to winning the war. He adds that even though it's brave for someone to die in battle, it is something anyone can do. It's more difficult to stay alive and work hard to do the things you want to accomplish in your life.

Alexander knows helping George is a really great chance for him to do something people will remember him for, and he is not going to give up his **shot**! He starts thinking of lots of ways to help George with the problems he's having in the war: Alexander's friends can help,[4] they will get people to spy on the British, he will ask Congress for more money and supplies, and the troops can learn how to do surprise attacks.

Alexander is so excited to be able to help win the war. He believes if he does a good job, he will "**rise up**" in life, which means he will get to have a higher **social status**. It also means people will think of him as being someone really important, because they will know who he is and how he helped defeat the British. He's thrilled and proud to be George's **right-hand man**—his biggest helper and close friend.

---

1 This was actually called the "Battle of Long Island," but it happened in the place we call "Brooklyn" today. There were lots and lots of battles, or fights, during the war, but this was the biggest one. It happened on

August 27th, 28th, and 29th in 1776.

2 They got on boats and rowed across the river to another part of New York called Manhattan. It took a long time to row everybody across, and some of the soldiers were still crossing the river when the sun started coming up. Thankfully, there was a *really* thick fog in the morning that made it so the British couldn't see them retreating. All 9,000 troops from the Continental Army made it safely to Manhattan!

3 Alexander, Hercules, and others actually stole the cannons in 1775, not during this battle in 1776. And while they were doing that, the British troops were attacking them the whole time from their ships!

4 Alexander actually met John and Lafayette after he joined the war—he didn't already know them when he first started helping George. He did already know Hercules, and he did come up with the idea for Hercules to spy on the British at his tailor shop.

9. A WINTER'S BALL
Aaron and Alexander think all the ladies like them

Aaron wonders how Alexander keeps getting so much attention and fame. He's also a bit jealous that Alexander is becoming such good friends with George Washington, because he is a very powerful person.[1] Aaron says Alexander still really wishes he could fight in a battle, instead of helping with the war by writing for George.

Aaron admits that Alexander is a very good writer, but he says he is just as good as Alexander at **flirting** with lots of ladies. Flirting means saying funny, sweet, or romantic things to try to get someone to like you. The two men start talking about the Schuyler sisters, and how if they could marry one, they would become rich. Alexander brags that it won't be hard to get one of the sisters to marry him, he just has to choose *which* one he wants.

---

1 Aaron says Alexander is "sitting next to the right hand of the father," because Alexander is considered George's "right hand man," and George is thought of as a "father" of the United States. Christians also say this about Jesus: They believe that ever since Jesus went up to heaven, he sits at the right hand, or right side, of God, who is also called "the Father."

10. HELPLESS
Eliza falls in love with Alexander

Eliza is at a fancy party with her sisters, and some soldiers are there, too. When she sees Alexander walk into the room, she falls in love with him right away. Her heart feels like it is jumping out of her chest with excitement. She is a little shy, and she's not sure what to say to him or how to get his attention, but she tells her sister Angelica that she really likes him a lot.

Angelica walks over to Alexander. She talks to him for a few minutes and then brings him over to meet Eliza. Eliza is nervous. She likes him so much, she feels helpless—she doesn't know what to say or what to do! She thinks Alexander's eyes are incredibly handsome,[1] and when he looks at her, her heart feels like it completely melts into a puddle of love. Eliza thanks Alexander for his service in the war, and he flirts with her, saying it's all worth it because now he is getting to meet her.

Fast-forward to one week later. Eliza and Alexander are writing lots of love letters back and forth to each other, which is the only way they can talk to each other when they aren't together.[2] Angelica says Alexander is so wonderful, she wishes Eliza would share him with her.[3]

Just a few weeks after meeting at the ball, Alexander asks Eliza's father for permission to marry her. Eliza is really anxious about what her father will say, but she knows Alexander is so smart that if there's something he wants, he will make it happen. She is SO excited when her father says "Yes," they can get married. Alexander is officially "hers" now—she gets to have him all to herself.

Note: Loving someone does not mean they *belong* to you, but this idea comes up a few times in the story.

Alexander warns Eliza that he doesn't have any money, or land, or fame, but he does have honor and he is very intelligent. He loves how it feels to be part of her family, and he talks a little bit about the difficult life he had growing up as a child. He says he will always love her and will make sure she never feels helpless again, as long as he's alive. They get married,[4] and Alexander feels like he is truly becoming a new man—a man who's not struggling anymore, a man who doesn't have to keep trying so hard to be loved and accepted.

———————

1 Many people who knew Alexander wrote about his bright and sparkling violet-blue eyes.

2 The telephone doesn't get invented until almost 100 years later! Texting came a long time after that.

3 Angelica and Alexander had a very special and close friendship their whole lives. Angelica did make a joke in a letter to Eliza, saying she wished she would share Alexander with her, but it was many years later. Maybe Angelica meant it would be fun to pretend he was her husband, or maybe she meant she would like to have him come visit her so she could spend time with him.

4 Here's an actual timeline of Alexander and Eliza's courtship leading up to their wedding:
- February 1780: They meet
- February or March 1780: Alexander asks Eliza's father for permission to marry her
- April 1780: Philip and Catherine Schuyler, Eliza's parents, give Alexander permission to marry Eliza
- December 14, 1780: They get married

II. SATISFIED

uh-oh, Angelica loves Alexander, too

At Eliza and Alexander's wedding, Angelica gives a toast—and it's not the kind of toast people eat. A **toast** is what it's called when someone stands up and says nice things about someone else in front of everyone. Angelica gives a toast to the bride and groom, and she reminds Eliza she will always be there for her, no matter what. She says she hopes Eliza and Alexander are always **satisfied** in their life together, which means she hopes they are happy.

Then, in her mind, Angelica **rewinds**, or goes back, to the time when she first meets Alexander. She says she will always remember that moment for the rest of her life. Right when she met him, she could see how smart he was. And—just like what happened to Eliza—Angelica fell in love right away. Her mind was so distracted by the strong feelings she had for him, that for a second she couldn't even remember her name! **(Pretty crazy and intense, isn't it?)**

When they meet, Alexander flirts with Angelica. He tells her she is just like him, because he has never been satisfied with his accomplishments in life. He thinks Angelica feels the same way about her own life, so he is trying to show her that he is a lot like her. It might also be his way of saying he's sure Angelica has never met someone who is equally as smart as she is.

Angelica asks Alexander where his family is from, but he feels embarrassed about being from a family that didn't have a lot of money, isn't famous, and didn't live in the colonies, especially because the Schuyler family is very rich and famous in New York.[1] He says it's not important and assures her he is going to do incredible things and make a great life for himself.

Angelica talks to Alexander for a few minutes and thinks, "Wow, this guy is as smart and witty as I am, I've never met anyone like him before!" She feels an exciting connection[2] with him and thinks she might fall in love with him.[3] But then she looks over at Eliza and sees that she is already helplessly in love with him. She realizes three things right away that help her make up her mind NOT to try to marry Alexander.

First, it's her job, as the oldest daughter, to marry someone rich—a man who will give her a good life, help take care of her family, and keep her family's important place in society.[4]

Second, she can tell that Alexander is trying to flirt with her because her family is wealthy and important. She knows if Alexander marries someone important, it helps *him* become more important and part of a higher **social class**. She wants someone who likes her for who she is, not her social status.

Third, Angelica loves her sister very much and would do absolutely anything for her. She knows Eliza would also do anything to make Angelica happy, including give up the man she just fell madly in love with, to let Angelica have him instead. So, if Angelica told Eliza that *she* loves Alexander, Eliza would let her have him, and she would say it's fine, but on the inside she would be heartbroken. Angelica doesn't want to be the reason Eliza doesn't get to marry the man she loves, so she keeps her feelings a secret. Her love for her sister is more important to her than the feelings she has for Alexander.

Angelica often wonders how different everything would be if she hadn't figured out all that stuff about Alexander so quickly. What might have happened if she did not decide to let Eliza have him? Even though it makes her heart hurt not to be the one who marries Alexander, Angelica tries to focus on being happy that Eliza is happy. She is grateful she still gets to have Alexander in her life, as her sister's husband. But deep down in her heart, she knows Alexander will probably never be completely satisfied, and neither will she.

---

1 A long time ago (and sometimes even today), people could guess a lot about you if they knew where your family was from. They could guess how much schooling you had and what people you probably knew. They could also figure out whether you had a lot of money, some money, or not a lot at all.

That's why Alexander doesn't answer Angelica's question. He doesn't want her to figure out all those things about him and then decide not to give him a chance to impress her and maybe win her heart.

2 Angelica mentions Benjamin Franklin, a key, and a kite in this song. Benjamin was a "**founding father**" of the United States. He believed lightning had electricity in it, so he did an experiment with a kite during a thunderstorm. He proved it was true!

When Angelica describes how she felt when she met Alexander, she is saying it felt like an electric spark in her heart, like lightning—she was very excited and surprised by her feelings.

3 It didn't really happen this way. Angelica was already married and had two children when she met Alexander.

4 During this time, women got their **social status** from their husbands. When a woman married, any gifts her family gave as a thank you to the husband for marrying her (called a **dowry**) became her husband's property. If he was wealthy, this would be added to the money and value he had, and then it would be passed down to their children. If he was *not* wealthy, there was no way to know what might happen to the gifts or money. He might spend it all.

Angelica's family was already at the very top in social status, so she needed to marry someone who would not waste her family's money. Also, she did have three brothers and two more sisters who are not in the story.

12. THE STORY OF TONIGHT (REPRISE)

Alexander celebrates with his friends, and Aaron has a secret love

Alexander's friends tease him about how surprised they are that he really got married—they didn't think he would want to choose just one person to love and be with for his whole life. They joke about how, now that he's married, he will never be completely free again, but he also will not be poor anymore.

Aaron comes in to congratulate Alexander on his marriage. None of Alexander's friends like Aaron, but Alexander tells him to ignore them. He congratulates Aaron on becoming a **Lieutenant Colonel**[1] (*pronounced "loo-ten-ent ker-nel"*), which is someone who is in charge of soldiers. Alexander says he wishes *he* could be in charge of soldiers in the war, too, instead of writing for George. Aaron points out that Alexander is actually pretty lucky, because George depends on Alexander for a lot of things, which makes him very important.

John teases Aaron by saying he heard Aaron has a special lady he secretly loves. Alexander tells his friends to leave, so they do. Aaron explains that the woman he loves is already married to a British officer. Alexander can't imagine not going after something—or someone—he wants, no matter what gets in his way. He tells Aaron he will never understand him, and that Aaron should do whatever he can to be with her—that there's no reason to wait.

---

1 Aaron became a Lieutenant Colonel in 1777, three years before Alexander and Eliza's wedding.

13. WAIT FOR IT
Aaron will wait patiently to get what he really wants

Aaron is alone, and he tells us about the woman he loves, Theodosia. But there's a problem: she's married to a British officer, who is in charge of part of the British army.[1] Aaron explains that love happens to people, whether they are good people or bad people, and it's not something that can be controlled—it just happens.

Aaron is willing to wait for Theodosia to not be married anymore, because he really loves her and wants to be with her, and she really likes him back. They just can't be together yet, since she is married.[2] Unlike Alexander, who tends to jump in right away to try and get whatever he wants, Aaron thinks it's better to wait patiently. He doesn't give up, and he doesn't forget about what he wants. Instead, he believes there will be a moment that is just right... and *that* is when he will get what—or who—he wants.

Aaron says that when his mother and father died,[3] he wasn't sure what to do. All he knew was that he wanted to protect their **legacy**. He

Legacy: This word comes up a lot in "Hamilton." It basically means what people remember about you after you are gone.

does not want to mess it up by doing something wrong that makes people think badly about his family.

Aaron thinks about how so many people in his life who mattered to him have died. He believes there must be a reason he is still be alive, and he thinks it must be so he can do something great. Whatever great thing he is meant to do with the life he has been given, he will wait patiently for it to happen.

The only thing Aaron believes he can truly control in life is himself, which is why he is very careful about what he says and does. It's also why he tells Alexander and his friends that it is best *not* to tell people what you believe in. To Aaron, it's better to hide your thoughts and ideas until you find out what other people think.

Aaron thinks about Alexander a lot, and how different he is from Aaron. He wonders what it is like to be Alexander, who takes a lot of risks, is always trying to prove how smart he is, and wants people to listen to everything he says.[4] He imagines it must be exhausting to be Alexander, working so hard *all* the time.

Aaron cannot understand how Alexander is so successful, when he just does whatever he wants without worrying about what other people might think. Even though Aaron is jealous of Alexander's success, he decides he likes his own way of approaching life better. He is willing to wait for his chance to be great, even if it takes a little bit longer.

1 The woman Aaron loved, Theodosia, was married to her husband for 18 years before he died in 1781 from injuries he got in the war. She met Aaron in 1778, and they got married in July of 1782.

Even though her husband served in the British army and she was friendly with the British, Theodosia also spent time with a lot of important Patriots, like George. She even allowed the Continental Army to use her family's home as their headquarters during the war at one point.

2 In a letter Theodosia wrote to Aaron, she said she was sure that other people noticed how much she really liked him, because she gave him much more attention than she gave anyone else.

3 Sadly, both of Aaron's parents *and* his grandparents all died a year apart from each other, when he was only two years old.

4 Alexander is working hard to make a *new* legacy from the one he got from his parents. He wants to be remembered for doing great things, not for being a poor orphan. One way Aaron is different from Alexander is that he wants to *protect* the legacy he got from his parents. It is also why he is very careful about his choices.

14. STAY ALIVE

The war is getting pretty scary

The war is getting really, really hard. Alexander is writing everything for George, who is afraid the colonies might lose the war soon. The soldiers have no food, and they are tired. The **merchants**, or store owners, don't help the soldiers because they will only accept British money.[1]

George decides the only way they can win the war is to kind of change the rules. The British soldiers are better trained, better fed, and have better supplies, which makes it really hard to beat them in a regular battle in the daytime. Instead, George says they are going to attack the British at nighttime to surprise them, so George's army has a better chance of winning. He hopes this will make Great Britain decide the war is costing too much money and too many people, and they will quit.

Many soldiers die during the battles, fighting bravely for America's freedom. Alexander and his friends do everything they can to help the colonies win the war. Hercules goes back to New York,[2] Lafayette asks France to send ships to help them win the war, and John and Alexander write about ending slavery[3] and keep fighting against the British. During all of this, Alexander asks George over and over if he can have a **command**, which means be in charge of some soldiers. Every time he asks, George says "No."

Instead, George puts someone named Charles Lee in charge, making him a General. But Charles ends up not being a good leader at all. He doesn't listen to George's orders to attack— instead, he tells his soldiers to **retreat**, or turn away. George replaces Charles with Lafayette, and the battle ends up in a tie, right before the Continental Army was about to lose.

Charles is angry and offended that George didn't let him stay in charge.[4] To get back at him, Charles starts telling everybody that George is a terrible General. Alexander gets really mad at Charles for saying so many mean things that aren't even true, but George tells Alexander to leave him alone and focus on the war instead.

John is also upset about the lies Charles says about George. He decides since Alexander isn't allowed to challenge Charles to a fight, he will do it.[5]

---

1 The Continental Congress printed its own money, and it was not very valuable. So an American dollar was only worth a few cents, which is why many people would only accept British money, which was still worth the amount it was supposed to be.

2 Hercules was actually in New York the whole time, working at his tailor shop, spying on the British, and sharing the secrets he discovered with Army leaders.

3 Alexander did write some papers against slavery, but he never made it the focus of his work like John did.

4 Charles got in big trouble for what he did during this battle, and he wasn't allowed to be part of the army for a year. He said lots of nasty things about George and Alexander, and he ended up not ever fighting in the war again.

5 In real life, John was so upset about what Charles said about George that he asked Alexander to write a response proving Charles wrong, the same way Alexander did when Samuel Seabury wrote his **pamphlets**.

15. TEN DUEL COMMANDMENTS
The rules for a duel[1]

John, Alexander, Charles, and Aaron are all together reviewing the rules for a **duel**.

John challenged Charles to a duel because of the lies Charles said about George—even though George already told Alexander to let it go and not fight with Charles.

Duel: At this time in history, dueling was very common. This is how it worked: if someone said something really bad about someone else, it was called insulting that person's "honor." The insulted person would challenge the person who said the mean things to a duel. That was his way of saying, "That was really nasty what you said about me, so you better apologize."

The whole point of a duel was actually to try to AVOID fighting. It was meant to help people work out their arguments before it ever turned into a fight. (The fights usually involved weapons.)

There were LOTS of rules about how to duel. Most of the time no one got hurt, because the person who said the mean thing would apologize. But sometimes people did get hurt, and sometimes they even died.

1. apologize

First, the challenger—the one who is upset about what the other person said—"**demands satisfaction**," which means asks for an apology. If the other person apologizes, it's over.

2. seconds

If he doesn't apologize, each person chooses a friend to help, who is called his "second." In this duel, Alexander is John's second, and Aaron is Charles' second.[2]

3. negotiate

The "seconds" try to end the argument without any fighting, by getting one or both men to let it go or apologize. If they can't reach a peaceful solution, then they decide on a time and a place for the duel to happen.[3] Most duels end at this point.

4. weapons & doctor

They choose their weapons and find a doctor who will agree to be at the duel in case someone gets hurt. The doctor faces the other way at the duel so he can honestly say he didn't see what happened. (Dueling was illegal in most places, so this way the doctor wouldn't get in trouble for being part of it.)

5. dawn

Duels usually happen at **dawn**, when the sun starts to rise. One reason is so both people have a chance to calm down overnight and might decide to apologize instead of fighting.

1	2	3	4	5
Ask for an apology	Find a friend to be your second	Friends negotiate then decide details	Get weapons and a doctor	Arrive at dawn

6. write

Each person in the duel writes a letter to let their family know what they are doing. This way if they do die, their family will receive the letter and find out what happened.

7. pray

Once the **duelists**[4]—the people who are getting ready to duel—and their seconds arrive, the duelists usually ask God for forgiveness for the mistakes they have made in their life.

8. negotiate again

The seconds have one last chance to talk to each other and try to reach a peaceful ending without any fighting.

> *Alexander and Aaron agree that duels are kind of silly. But Alexander says Charles has to "pay" for what he said, since he refused to apologize. And a lot of soldiers died because Charles didn't listen to George and told his men to leave the battle. So, the duel is going to happen.*

9. look

The two duelists look each other in the eye and try their best to be brave.[5]

10. paces & fire

The last rule is that the two duelists usually walk ten **paces**, or steps, away from each other. Then they turn back around and **fire**, or shoot, their guns at each other.[6]

6	7	8	9	10
Write letters to family	Pray, asking God to forgive	Negotiate one last time	Look right at each other	Walk 10 paces, turn, and fire

Dueling was considered a way for men to defend their honor or reputation—by proving they were willing to die for it. **Seems pretty silly, doesn't it?**

-----

1 There were actually a lot more than ten rules for duels, but these are the basic rules combined together to make ten.

2 In real life, Aaron wasn't actually Charles' second. A man named Evan Edwards was his second.

3 The person who was challenged to the duel was the one who got to choose the weapons as well as the time and place for the duel.

4 Duelists were almost always men, but there were a few times in history when women dueled. There is no record of women ever dueling in colonial America or the United States.

5 According to the rules for a duel, you were not allowed to aim into the air. If both people agreed to the duel and could not settle it in advance with an apology, then they had to be willing to actually participate in the duel.

6 To find out what happens in this duel between Charles and John, see the next song!

16. MEET ME INSIDE
George is really mad at Alexander

At the duel, John hurts Charles, and Charles "**yields**." That means he wants the duel to be over and admits John won.[1] George happens to see them all and asks, "What is going on here?!" He tells Charles that even though they don't agree with each other, George never wanted anyone to duel Charles because of the bad things Charles said about him.

As everyone leaves, George angrily tells Alexander to meet him inside. Alexander knows George is very upset about what he did. He tries to explain that he really didn't like the mean lies Charles said about George. George explains that when their own team starts fighting with each other, it upsets people in the colonies who support their side in the war, which makes even bigger problems for everyone, especially George.

Trying to show Alexander he cares about him and just wants him to be careful, George calls Alexander "son." He is not Alexander's father, but he calls him that to mean "young man I care about." Alexander does not like being called "son," because to him it means George thinks he is like a kid.

Alexander still really wants to be in charge of soldiers in the war. He thinks it is his best chance to be remembered, make more money, and have a better life. He wants this *very* much. He has already asked George about it a few times. Alexander begs George again. He says if he could be in charge of soldiers, he could get a higher **social status**, so people would think of him as more important than he is right now.

George warns Alexander that he could die if he fights in battle, and George needs him to stay alive. Alexander is very important to helping the colonies win the war, even though he is not leading soldiers on the battlefield. George reminds Alexander that Eliza also wants him to stay safe and alive. He calls Alexander "son" again, and this time Alexander gets really angry about it. He talks back to George, which is considered very disrespectful. So George orders him to go home, kicking him out of the war.[2]

---

1 After Charles got hurt, John started to help him, but Charles said he was not hurt as badly as he thought he was at first. Then, Charles said he wanted to have a second round in the duel, and John agreed to it. But Alexander and Evan Edwards (Charles' "second" in real life) convinced them to be done with the duel.

2 In reality, Alexander decided to quit his job as George's "right hand man"—George didn't send him home. There was a situation where George asked to talk to Alexander about something, and Alexander said he would be there right away. George went upstairs to his room. Alexander handed someone a letter, and on his way to the staircase he ran into Lafayette. They spoke for a minute or two.

When he got upstairs to see what George wanted to talk to him about, George was surprisingly very angry with Alexander for making him wait. He said it was disrespectful. Alexander said he didn't mean to be disrespectful, but because George thought he was, Alexander would leave.

17. THAT WOULD BE ENOUGH

Eliza wants Alexander to share more of his thoughts and feelings with her

Alexander goes home and sees that Eliza is pregnant! He is very surprised they are going to have a baby. Eliza says she wrote George a letter to tell him about it a month ago and begged him to send Alexander home. Alexander is a little upset by this, because he really wanted to stay and be a hero in the war.[1] But Eliza just wants Alexander to be safe and stay alive so he can meet their child when he is born.[2]

Eliza points out how lucky they are to be alive, the same way she did earlier with her sisters in the city. She is so happy with their life together, she is grateful Alexander is alive, and she is very excited about having their first baby.

Alexander wants to be happy, but he is still worried about not being able to give Eliza the nice things she is used to having, since he still doesn't have a lot of money. Eliza assures him she doesn't need money or fancy things. Just having a life with Alexander is enough to make her completely happy.

Eliza wishes Alexander would share more about what he's thinking and feeling with her. She asks him to let her be a part of the story people will write about him someday, by letting her know him and support his dreams and goals, and be his partner in life. It's what she wants most, because she loves him so much. She also wants Alexander to feel that she is enough to make him happy, and that their family together is all he needs.

---

1 In this story, Alexander may also be upset Eliza told George about the baby but didn't tell Alexander right away. (But this part of the story didn't really happen this way. See note #2.)

2 Eliza didn't actually know if they were going to have a boy or a girl when she was pregnant. She also wasn't pregnant yet when Alexander left his job in the war and returned home.

18. GUNS AND SHIPS

Lafayette convinces George to bring Alexander back into the war

How does America win the war against the big, powerful British military? With help from Lafayette, a beloved war hero from France! He is a genius military leader who does a great job leading the American **troops** in battles against the British. He also helps a lot by asking France to send supplies. They send money[1], guns, and ships.

Lafayette tells George he thinks they can win the war in the battle at Yorktown coming up soon, but they will need Alexander's help to do it.[2] George admits he is right and says he needs his "right-hand man" to come back.

Lafayette suggests that George should hurry up and get Alexander to come back to the war right now, before it's over. And that's exactly what George does. He tells Alexander he can finally be in charge of a group of soldiers in a really important battle, which is what Alexander has wanted so badly for so long. George says if they all do a really good job in this surprise battle, they might even win the whole war!

---

1 John Laurens is actually the one who brought back a *lot* of money from France when he visited them to ask for help, along with a promise they would send even more money later. But Lafayette did get six ships and 6,000 soldiers from the King of France to help the colonies with the war.

2 Some people say Lafayette actually recommended a fellow Frenchman to lead this group of soldiers, but Alexander said he deserved to be in charge of them. George agreed with Alexander and let him lead the soldiers.

19. HISTORY HAS ITS EYES ON YOU
George gives Alexander advice about being a military leader

George is getting ready to give Alexander his first **command**, which means his first time being in charge of soldiers in the war. George says one of the first times he was in charge of soldiers in a battle, he made a really big mistake and a lot of people died.[1] He felt terrible, and he still thinks about it a lot, even though it was many years ago.

George knows people are watching him closely, waiting to see if he will make another big mistake or do something great. So far, he's been doing a really good job leading the Continental Army, but he knows it's important to think carefully about every choice he makes. People will remember him for what he does, whether it's good or bad.

George tells Alexander that when he was younger, he used to hope people would always remember him for being brave in battles. But he wishes someone would have told him you cannot control how people remember you or what they

> **Note:** The idea of not having control over what people remember about you after you are gone comes up a lot in "Hamilton." It is part of the theme, or idea, of legacy.

will think about you, especially after you are gone. He shares this powerful lesson with Alexander.

George says he knows Alexander can do great things, and he knows they can win the war. But he warns Alexander that people will be paying attention to the choices he makes and what happens next, for a long time after he is gone.

---

1 This happened at the Battle of Fort Necessity in 1754, when George had just become an army Colonel. This battle caused bad relationship problems between the British and the French. It is one of the main reasons the Seven Years' War, which is sometimes called the French and Indian War, started.

20. YORKTOWN (THE WORLD TURNED UPSIDE DOWN)
The last battle of the war

Alexander and Lafayette are excited to see each other at the Battle of Yorktown, and Lafayette is happy Alexander finally gets to be in command of **troops**. They are both proud to be fighting for America's freedom from Britain.

Lafayette says if they win this last battle and the war ends, he will go back to France to help his country get freedom from their King. Alexander says the colonies will support France in fighting for their independence, just like France helped the American Colonies so much in their war. They wish each other good luck and split up to lead their troops. Alexander is incredibly excited and proud to finally have his chance at glory and fame by leading an important battle.

Throughout his life, Alexander has often imagined how he might die, and he's wondering if it might happen in this battle. At first, he thinks that would be fine, because it's what he has always wanted. But then he remembers Eliza is waiting for him back home, *and* his son will be born soon. He realizes he really *doesn't* want to die, because he has so much to live for now.[1]

Alexander has a plan for the battle against the British. He makes all of his soldiers take the bullets out of their guns. Why? This way, none of their guns will accidentally shoot and give away their sneak attack. The plan works, and they defeat the British!

Alexander tells us what his friends are all doing during this time: **John** is working really hard in South Carolina,[2] trying to make it possible for 3,000 black enslaved people to earn their freedom by fighting in the war. **Lafayette** and his soldiers are waiting for the British troops in the exact spot where they try to escape.[3] **Hercules** is working as a tailor *and* a spy. He learns about the British troops' secret plans while he makes their clothes, and then he tells the Continental Army leaders everything.

The battle at Yorktown lasts for about a week. One morning, the Continental Army sees a British soldier waving a white handkerchief high in the air. In war, this is a way of saying, "We give up, you win." The battle is over, and the colonies have finally won their freedom from Britain![4] Both sides agree to the British surrender in writing, and the defeated British troops are allowed to leave and go home.

People everywhere in the colonies are **THRILLED** the war is over—they run out of their homes and shops, cheering and celebrating. They are finally free to start their own country. But sadly, this does not include freedom for enslaved people.[5]

As the British march away to return home, they are

incredibly shocked about what happened. How could they have lost the war? While they walk, they sing a song called "The World Turned Upside Down."[6] It is a way of saying the craziest thing they *never* thought could happen *did* just happen. It feels like the whole world just changed in a really big way... and it really did.

---

1 Alexander wrote a letter to Eliza afterward, telling her he was in a very risky situation, being in charge of an attack on the British. He knows he could have died. He tells Eliza not to worry because he won't be in this much danger again.

2 John was actually in the same battle with Alexander. He went back to his home state of South Carolina *after* the Battle of Yorktown.

3 This gets a little confusing, but Lafayette actually attacked the British at the same time in the same place Alexander did. The French navy was also there, blocking the British from escaping, but that wasn't what Lafayette was doing.

4 This battle wasn't officially the end of the war, but it basically was. There were no more big battles after this one.

- A few months after this battle, Britain's

Parliament decided they should stop fighting the
war.
- The first peace agreements were signed a few
months after that, in 1782.
- About a year later (1783), two years after
Yorktown, both sides signed the final peace
treaty, or agreement. Now the war was finally
officially over, and the American Colonies were
free from Britain.

5 The American Colonists who fought so hard for their
freedom from Britain won it, but they did not choose to
free the 500,000 people they forced to be slaves.

Some enslaved people were promised they would get
their freedom if they fought in the war. Some of them
did get their freedom after helping in the war, but
many of those promises were broken.

About 20,000 people who used to be enslaved left the
American Colonies with the British at the end of the
war, but some of them were sadly sold back into slavery.
Some states in the north made slavery illegal after the
war, but the southern states did not.

It is very sad that a country that fought so hard for
its freedom and talked so much about the importance of
independence did not choose to make all people free.
Instead, hundreds of thousands of people remained
enslaved and were forced to keep working for other

people without getting paid and without any freedom to leave.

6 No one knows if this is the song the British actually sang when they left, but it does explain how they probably felt!

"The World Turned Upside Down" was the name of a poem written more than one hundred years before the war, and there were some songs that included those words in them. But there is no record or **evidence**, which means proof, any of these were sung by the British as they left after losing the war.

21. WHAT COMES NEXT?
King George doesn't think the colonies can lead themselves

Back in England, King George is pretty shocked and also kind of sad Britain lost the war. He still thinks of the colonies as his girlfriend, but now it's clear they are not a couple anymore. He is also mad France helped them win the war.

King George wonders... "What's going to happen next? Do you know how hard it is to be in charge of a whole country?" He knows it is really hard work, and he doesn't think the colonies have any idea what they have gotten themselves into, now that they have won their freedom. There are a lot of hard choices to make, and it can be lonely when you are in charge. Not everyone is going to agree with what you do, and they may even get really mad and say mean things about you.

King George is basically telling the colonies, "Someday you are going to learn how hard it is to have your own country. And when you want to come back to me and be my girlfriend again, too bad. You missed your chance."

And guess what? He's right! It *is* really hard to decide how the country should work. But there are lots of people who will work as hard as they can to make sure they come up with a great plan.

———————————

22. DEAR THEODOSIA

Alexander and Aaron are very excited to be new fathers

Aaron sings a lullaby to his newborn daughter, Theodosia. She's named after her mother, the woman Aaron has loved for several years, who used to be married to a British officer.[1] The moment Aaron met his newborn baby girl, his whole world changed. She is the most important thing in his life now, and he will dedicate every day to giving her a wonderful life.[2]

Aaron wants the leaders of the newly formed country to do the best job they can at planning how the government will work. He has really big dreams for his daughter, Theodosia, and he wants to help make the country a great place for her to live in. He hopes she will be able to follow all of the dreams and goals she has for her life, because he loves her so much and wants her to be happy. Whatever she does, he is sure she will **blow everyone away**, which means she will amaze everyone.

Alexander also sings a lullaby to his newborn son, Philip.[3] Just like Aaron, becoming a father has made Alexander happier than he has ever felt before. Just looking at his baby boy melts his heart—especially when he smiles. Alexander thought he knew a lot about life, but everything changes for him when he becomes a father. Now he has new feelings, new responsibilities, and new dreams for his son's life, instead of just his own.

Both men grew up without their own fathers, which created a wound in each of their hearts. Aaron and Alexander promise they will always be there for their child and love them forever. They know they won't be perfect fathers, but they promise to do their very, very best. They're also going to work really hard to make sure this new country is a great one, where their children can dream big and do whatever amazing things they want to do when they grow up.

---

1 Aaron and the woman he loved, Theodosia, got married after her first husband died. (See Song #13 footnotes for more details.)

2 Aaron did work hard to give his daughter the best possible life. He made sure she had a great education, which is something not many girls had during this time. He adored her and wrote many letters to her whenever he was away from her.

3 Aaron's daughter and Alexander's son were both born shortly after the war. Philip Hamilton was born six months after the Battle of Yorktown, and Theodosia Burr was born two years after the battle.

23. NON-STOP

Alexander works so hard, he never stops

After the war, Alexander and Aaron both studied to become lawyers, and sometimes they work together. Alexander talks a lot in court, just like he always does. Aaron tells him, "You don't have to say so much. You can keep it simple and still get to the point." Aaron thinks the reason Alexander talks so much is to try to prove he's the smartest person in the room.

Aaron wonders to himself, "Alexander, why do you write so much?" It seems like Alexander writes every single day about the government and how he thinks it should work.

Alexander feels like he has done a really good job at being a lawyer, so now he wants to help work on the country's laws and **economy**, which means how money works. He is very excited when he gets invited to go to a big, special meeting called the Constitutional Convention. When it's his turn to talk at the meeting, he explains all of his ideas for how the government should work. His speech lasts *six hours*!

Late one night, Alexander visits Aaron at his home. He says it's for a really important reason. He asks Aaron to help him write some papers to explain and defend the new **Constitution**, which is the new set of rules for the country.[1] Alexander gives Aaron a lot of compliments as a way to try to convince him to help, like telling him he is really good at getting people to agree with his ideas without using a lot of words to do it. Aaron says, "No," he won't do it. He thinks the Constitution needs some fixing, and he's not sure if people will agree with it or not. He doesn't want to write papers trying to prove it is great, in case people don't like it.

Alexander admits that the Constitution is not perfect, but he believes it's a good start. He says they have to do *something* to get people to understand it and believe in it, so the country and the government can start to grow and develop. Aaron still says "Absolutely not" to writing the papers about the Constitution. Alexander is frustrated. He doesn't understand why Aaron was willing to fight for the colonies' independence from Britain but won't speak out to help make their new country a great one.

Alexander asks Aaron if he believes in the Constitution, and Aaron says of course he does.[2] So Alexander asks him again to help defend it. Aaron says he will wait to see what other people think about it first, before he stands up for it. So he does not help Alexander with his project.

Meanwhile, Angelica leaves to go to London with her husband,[3] and Eliza says she just wants a tiny bit of Alexander's time. She wishes spending time with her would be enough to make him happy.

But Alexander is still very focused on making sure people understand the Constitution and support it. He decides to ask

James Madison and John Jay to help him, and they agree. The papers they all write are called *The Federalist Papers*. The three of them make a plan to write 25 papers, with all of them writing about the same amount. But there was so much they wanted to say, they ended up writing **85 papers** instead! Wow! Alexander wrote *way* more than either John or James: he wrote 51 of them![4] Everyone is amazed at how Alexander can possibly write **so much**. It's like he never, ever stops.

George Washington is chosen to be the first president of the country, and he asks Alexander to help him. George is choosing people to be part of something called his **Cabinet**, where each person is in charge of a different part of running the country. He asks Alexander to be the leader of the Treasury department, which is in charge of all of the country's money. Alexander is very excited and says, "Yes!"

Working for George means Alexander will be even busier than he was before. Eliza doesn't want Alexander to go,[5] but Alexander uses her words to show her what a great opportunity this is for him, pointing out that they are so lucky to be alive at this time in history. It's such a special time in the country, and Alexander will get to be a really important part of figuring out how it's all going to work. Eliza feels helpless again, but it is not in a happy way from falling in love, like it was before. This time, she feels helpless because no matter what she says, she cannot convince Alexander to stay with her, which is all she wants.

Everyone has their own things they are thinking about Alexander as they watch him work so hard. Angelica still thinks he will never be satisfied. Eliza is starting to realize that is probably true, no matter what job he gets or how great their family is. George reminds Alexander that people—now and far into the future—will be paying close attention to the things Alexander does, especially since he's going to be in charge of the country's money. Aaron still wants to know why Alexander thinks he's the smartest person alive. He has a feeling it will get Alexander into big trouble someday.

Alexander knows this is his big chance to help decide what the country will become. He says he is not going to throw away his **shot**, which means he is not going to give up this opportunity.

1 There's no **evidence** Alexander ever asked Aaron for help with this project. He *did* ask a few other people to help, but probably not Aaron.

2 We don't know for sure what Aaron thought about the Constitution. He was part of a group of people who did **not** like the Constitution, but we don't know what he actually thought about it.

3 Angelica and her husband lived in France and England for 14 years. She visited the United States a few times before she, John, and their children moved back to New York.

Fun Facts: Angelica's husband, John Barker Church, actually dueled Aaron Burr in 1799. Both men missed their first shots. John then apologized for what he had said about Aaron, and it was over. Also, when Angelica met and married John, he was using the fake name "John B. Carter," because he was trying to hide from people he owed money to.

4 The Federalist Papers were originally called "The Federalist." All 85 of the essays, or papers, were published in the newspaper **anonymously**, which means the authors' names were not on them. The writers used the name "Publius" as a pretend author name instead. Because Alexander and James worked together on some of the papers, we are not absolutely sure exactly how many each of them wrote. But we do know Alexander wrote a lot more than John or James did.

5 Alexander didn't actually have to *go* anywhere. During this time, the United States **capital**, which is the place where most people in the country's government work, was in New York City, where Alexander lived. Today, the capital is in Washington, D.C., more than 200 miles away from New York City.

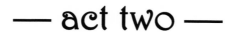

— act two —

24. WHAT'D I MISS?
Thomas Jefferson returns to the United States

♪ **Musical Note:** This song sounds a lot different from all the other songs in the show. It is slower and more relaxed. The style is called **funk**, which started in the 1960s but really became popular in the 1970s. It is a combination of other types of music, called soul, jazz, and R+B (rhythm + blues).

This "groovy" style of music is a way to show that Thomas is a little bit older than Alexander and his friends, because his music is from an older time. It also shows that he isn't caught up with what happened while he was gone—he missed a lot of things.

It's 1789, the year George becomes the very first president of the United States of America.[1] Aaron gives away a little bit of the story by mentioning some of the things Alexander is going to do, and also what happens because of those things. Then, Aaron introduces someone named Thomas Jefferson and explains that Thomas and Alexander do not get along very well. They disagree on a lot of things about how the country should work.

Thomas was in Paris, France for a few years after the war. While he was there, he helped Lafayette write a document for France declaring their independence, just like the colonies had done. Now, Thomas has just returned home to Monticello, the name of his house in Virginia, where he has work he wants to do.[2] When he arrives, he sees a letter from George asking him to be part of his Cabinet as the Secretary of State. His job will be to talk with people from other countries, and to ask them for help and give them help, depending on what the president wants him to do.

Thomas is pretty excited about this new job[3]. He goes to New York City to be part of George's Cabinet. When he gets there, his friend James Madison is upset. James says Thomas needs to help him stop Alexander's plan for the country's money.[4] He explains that Alexander's plan gives the government way too much control, which he doesn't think is a good thing for Southern farmers. So, before Thomas even has a chance to start his new job, he finds out there is already a lot of arguing going on about how the country should work.

George walks into the room to greet Thomas, and Thomas meets Alexander for the first time. He has been gone such a long time, and he starts to realize he has a bit of catching up to do.

------

1 Between the time the war ended in 1783, and the time George Washington became the first president of the United States in 1789, there were a few people who were called "president of the Continental Congress" or "president of the Congress." But that job wasn't at all the same as the president of the United States. Those leaders had almost no power and mostly just signed documents about decisions made by all of Congress.

Also, the way the president was chosen at this time worked a lot differently than it does today. Only some states let the people vote to choose the president. Other states chose a few people to be "Electors," and they got to decide who the state would vote for.

2 Thomas is talking about working on his house he was remodeling, and also about working on his home country, the United States. It took 15 years to build Monticello, and when he got back from France he spent 13 more years changing and adding on to it.

3 Actually, Thomas really liked being the ambassador to France, but he said he would take whichever job George wanted him to do. George told Thomas to decide which one he wanted, and he chose to be Secretary of State.

4 Thomas and Alexander actually got along pretty well during their first year or so in George's Cabinet. It was when Alexander was creating his plan for the country's money that they really started to disagree… a *lot.*

25. CABINET BATTLE #1

Thomas and Alexander argue about Alexander's plan for the country's money

George is hosting a Cabinet meeting. It's a meeting where the **Cabinet** members—his advisors—discuss the decisions they are trying to make. In today's meeting, they are talking about Alexander's plan for the country's money. Part of his plan includes having the **federal government** be in charge of paying back the money each state owes, which is called their **debts**. It also includes creating a national bank where all of the country's money can be kept.

Federal government: The part of government that is for the whole country, as one big group. It is sometimes called "central government." They make decisions or laws that affect everyone in the country. For other laws, each state gets to make its own decisions.

Thomas does not agree with Alexander's plan. He starts by quoting the Declaration of Independence, which he reminds everyone he wrote,[1] as a way to show that he's pretty smart and knows the best way for the country to work. He says Alexander's money plan is terrible. He especially doesn't like that it seems to help New York the most, where Alexander lives. He thinks that is a little suspicious.

Thomas explains that Alexander's plan hurts all of the states that don't owe any debt, because now the people in those states would have to help the *other* states by paying more **taxes**, which means extra money that goes toward helping everyone. Thomas doesn't think this is fair. He says southern states like Virginia, where he's from, grow and make things themselves, so they didn't have to borrow any money for the war. They don't owe anyone any debt, so why should they have to help pay for other states' debts?

Alexander tells Thomas running a country is harder than just imagining it and writing about it, like Thomas did with the Declaration of Independence. Alexander explains that his plan helps make the whole country better and stronger. If everyone pays a little bit extra, the country can pay back all of the money the states owe to other countries and can start working on building a strong **economy**.

Alexander calls Thomas a "slaver," because Thomas had a *lot* of **enslaved people** he forced to work for him. He adds that the reason Virginia doesn't owe any money is because a lot of people there don't spend any money paying their workers. Instead, they have enslaved people they force to do most of the work for them for free. He also points out that Thomas doesn't get to talk about the war, because he was out having fun and relaxing in France while Alexander and others were risking their lives here at home.[2]

As Alexander continues talking, he starts to get a bit nasty. When he calls Thomas and James mean names, George tells him to stop and asks everybody to take a quick break. George reminds Alexander that if he wants his plan for the country's money to actually happen, he needs to get enough votes from people to support it. He tells Alexander to figure out a way to make a **compromise**, or deal, to convince people to agree with his plan. George warns Alexander that if he isn't able to do that, then he will probably lose his job as Secretary of the Treasury.

---

1 Thomas wrote the very first draft, or version, of the Declaration of Independence. He asked John Adams and Ben Franklin to make changes if they wanted, and they made a few small changes. Then they gave it to Congress, who also made some changes. It was officially approved and accepted by Congress on July 4, 1776, which is why Americans celebrate Independence Day on that day every year.

2 Thomas was not really in France during the war. He

did not go until a year after the war was over. During the war, he was part of Virginia's government and later became the state's **governor**, which is sort of like the president, except the governor is the leader of one state instead of the whole country.

Thomas actually ran away when the British started to come near his home. He was able to get away, but while he was gone the British set fire to the entire state capital and burned it down.

26. TAKE A BREAK
Eliza and Angelica ask Alexander to join them on vacation

♪ Musical Note: The music and some of the words, or lyrics, to the song Philip and Eliza sing are the same as the duel countdown music from "Ten Duel Commandments" and two more songs coming up.

Philip is playing piano with his mother, Eliza, and counting to nine in French. Alexander is at his desk in another room. He's writing a letter to Angelica, complaining about how Thomas and James don't like his money plan and think he's annoying. Alexander and Angelica both say they miss each other very much and wish they didn't have a whole ocean separating them.

Eliza calls to Alexander from the other room, asking him to take a break. It's Philip's birthday, and he has a special surprise he is excited to show his father. Alexander goes into the room they are in, and Philip recites a fun poem he wrote. Alexander loves it and is very proud of his son. [1]

Eliza asks Alexander to take a vacation with them over the summer to her father's house in upstate New York, north of the city. He says he will think about it. Angelica writes another letter to Alexander, talking about how important it is for him to keep working hard to figure out how he can get Thomas to agree to his plan. She adds that she has been really distracted by the way Alexander wrote her name in his last letter to her. She wonders whether or not he meant to call her "My dearest." Does he mean out of all the people he knows, she is actually the one person who is dearest to him? Even more than her sister, Eliza?[2] She can't stop thinking about it.

Angelica changes the subject and excitedly tells Alexander she's coming back to the United States from Europe, where she lives now. She really hopes he will come to her father's house to visit her and to spend some time with his family.

Time skips ahead. Angelica arrives at Alexander and Eliza's house. They are all very excited to see each other, and the sisters ask Alexander one last time to please come with them on a vacation upstate. He reminds them he has to keep working on his plan until he convinces Congress to agree with it. He says he cannot take a break.

---

1 In his rap, Philip says he wants a little brother. He actually already had two little brothers by the time he was nine, Alexander and James Alexander, in addition to his little sister, named Angelica. Alexander and Eliza had four *more* children after that (three more boys and one more girl), for a total of eight kids!

2 An explanation of the comma: If Alexander had written "My dearest Angelica," with a comma after her name, that would be just a very normal, common way to start a letter back then. But if he really meant to write it the way he did, with a comma after "dearest" ("My dearest, Angelica"), it would mean that out of everyone in the world, Angelica is the one who is **dearest** to him—the most special to his heart.

How they both used commas in their letters to each other: It might have actually been Angelica who first put a sneaky comma in a letter to Alexander. In 1787, she wrote "Indeed my dear, Sir…." Alexander teased her about the comma and said he assumed it was a mistake but hoped it wasn't. Then he signed his letter "Adieu ma chere, soeur" which is French for "Farewell my dear, sister." So… he put in a sneaky comma, too.

Back in the 1700s, punctuation and spelling rules were just starting to be created. So a lot of people used them however they wanted. And that means we are left with a mystery about whether Angelica meant to be sneaky or not!

27. SAY NO TO THIS
Alexander meets a woman named Maria and makes a bad choice

Alexander is working really, really hard on his plan for how the country's money should work, and he isn't sleeping much at all. Eliza and Angelica are both at their father's home upstate[1] with the Hamilton kids, and Alexander is feeling lonely and tired.

Maria Reynolds (*pronounced "Muh-ry-uh"*) walks up to Alexander's house. She tells him her husband has not been treating her nicely, and now he has left her. She says she came to visit Alexander because she thought he might be willing to help her.

> **Note:** This song is kind of a grown-up one. It's mostly about how when people get married, they make a promise not to kiss anyone else. A grown-up might want to explain it to you themselves, or they might not really want to talk about it a lot, since it's not a situation kids get in.

Alexander offers to loan her money and gives her $30.[2] He walks her to her home a block away, and she says she wants to kiss him. He's married, and he knows he shouldn't kiss anyone except Eliza. He wants to say "No," but he says he just can't stop himself. (Of course, he actually *could* stop himself from doing it, but he doesn't make that choice.)

Even though Alexander knows it's wrong, he chooses to keep visiting Maria, and they kiss many times. Not being faithful to his wife is called having an **affair**.

After about a month,[3] Alexander receives a letter from James Reynolds, Maria's husband. In the letter, James says he knows what Alexander has been doing. He says if Alexander doesn't pay him a lot of money to keep it a secret, James is going to tell Eliza about it.

Alexander is **very** upset. He asks Maria if she was trying to trick him the whole time, just so she and James could get money from him. She claims she doesn't know about her husband sending Alexander a letter. She begs him to just give James what he wants—money—so she and Alexander can keep spending time together.[4] Alexander is angry with himself for getting into this messy situation, but he decides to pay James *and* keep visiting Maria.

---

1 This part of the story squishes timing a little bit. In real life, Eliza and the children were still home when Maria first came to the Hamiltons' house and Alexander first kissed her.

2 In the 1790s, $30 was a lot of money. It was about the same as $800 today! That is a really big amount of money to give someone you have never met before.

3 Alexander actually got the first letter from James Reynolds in December, a few months after he started visiting Maria. Altogether, Alexander and Maria kept secretly visiting each other for about a year.

4 We don't really know for sure if Maria was trying to trick Alexander, or if James decided on his own to make Alexander pay him money to keep the secret. But most **historians**—people who study history—believe Maria was working with James to trick Alexander and get money from him.

28. THE ROOM WHERE IT HAPPENS
Aaron wants to be part of secret conversations

> ♪ **Musical Note:** You might notice that this song has a **lot** of different styles of music in it, which makes it really cool and fun. If you really love music and have learned a lot about it, you can probably find at least three different musical styles just in this one song!

Aaron is walking down the street. He sees Alexander and says "Hello." He tells Alexander about a man we haven't heard of, General Mercer, who died during the war and got to have a street in New York named after him. Aaron and Alexander joke about how they survived the war and are working hard to make the country great, but they didn't get to have a street named after them.[1]

Aaron asks Alexander how he's going to get Congress to agree to his plan for the states' debt. Alexander says he's going to take Aaron's advice by talking less and smiling more, if that is what he has to do for Congress to consider his plan. He has learned he has to listen and compromise in order to get what he wants.

James Madison stops by to get Alexander, who says goodbye to Aaron. He has been invited to a special dinner where he, James, and Thomas are all going to talk about Alexander's debt plan. Aaron feels left out and wishes he could be at the dinner, too.

Aaron tells us the short version of what happens at the dinner: The three men talk and agree on a **compromise**. Alexander gets to be in charge of how the country's debt and money

Note: One of the main ways people in government work is by talking a lot with each other and making deals, or compromises, where each person gets something their "side" or group wants.

will work, and James and Thomas get to have the country's capital be in their home state of Virginia.

Aaron explains that even though most people in the country don't know what actually happens in these secret conversations and compromises people in government make with each other, they definitely do happen.

Thomas shares his version of what he claims *really* happened. He says Alexander was right outside Washington's house when he saw Thomas and begged him for help with his plan. Thomas asked James to at least give Alexander a chance to tell them about his plan, even though they don't like Alexander or his plan.

James knows they will have to make a compromise. He tells Thomas he will ask Alexander to support moving the capital from New York to an area between Virginia and Maryland, along the Potomac River. And, in exchange for his help, James won't stop Congress from approving Alexander's debt plan.[2] This way they can all help each other get what they want.

The three of them go to the dinner and have their secret conversation. When it is over, Alexander feels like he got the better deal, because he gets to be in charge of how all the money for the whole country works. He reminds Aaron that you have to speak up about what you want, otherwise you won't get anything. Alexander wants to be part of creating something that will last a long time after he is gone—

something that will be part of his **legacy**.

Alexander asks Aaron what he wants. He reminds Aaron that if he doesn't stand for anything or say what he wants, he won't get anything and people won't be able to trust him. This is the same thing Alexander said to Aaron when they first met: he has to say what he wants and be willing to fight for it.

Aaron finally admits, in secret, what he truly wants: to be someone who gets to make big decisions, and to be part of the small group of people who have the most power. There's nothing he claims to actually believe in, or wants to support, or hopes to create. He just doesn't want to be left out, and he wants to have the same power Alexander, Thomas, James, and others have. And he's finally ready to go after what he wants.

---

1 Lin-Manuel said he was so excited to discover this fact, since he was always looking for words to rhyme with "Burr, sir." This story about General Mercer fits perfectly with the story of this song, since part of it is about **legacy**—the memories and stories people remember about you, and what you leave behind after you're gone.

2 What really happened at the dinner? We don't know for sure, because Thomas is the only one who wrote about it. But we know James *could* have stopped

Alexander's debt plan from being passed in Congress if he wanted to, by convincing more people to vote against it. And we know James and Thomas both wanted the capital to be closer to their home state of Virginia, not in New York, and that is what ended up happening. Virginia and Maryland both gave up a little bit of their land to make Washington, D.C. its own district in 1790. After that, it took ten years to build the capital, and that's where it has been ever since.

These three men didn't officially make the decisions about the debt plan and the capital, but they agreed to influence, or convince, people in Congress to agree to both parts of the deal. "The Compromise of 1790" is also called the "Dinner Table Bargain," and it got two bills passed: first, the "Residence Act," about where the capital would be, and then the "Assumption Bill," about the federal government **assuming**, or taking over, the states' debts.

And guess what? James didn't even vote for Alexander's "Assumption Bill." He actually voted **against** it! But he *did* make it easier for it to get passed, or approved, by not convincing his friends in Congress to vote against it, which is something he could have done. So, he didn't try to stop it from getting passed, but he also did not vote for it.

29. SCHUYLER DEFEATED
Alexander is upset with Aaron for taking Eliza's father's job

Alexander's son Philip is reading the newspaper. He is very surprised to read that his grandfather, Eliza's father, lost his job in the **Senate** (part of Congress) to Aaron Burr.

Alexander finds Aaron and is not happy with him. He asks, "When did you change your mind and start agreeing with the Democratic-Republican ideas about government?"[1] Aaron says he did it because it helped him get what he wanted—to be part of Congress.[2] Aaron also says it doesn't even matter if

The **Senate** is one part of Congress. It is the part where each state gets the same number (two) of people to represent the state.

The people in a state vote for who they want their **Senators** to be. Senators have their job for six years. After six years, the people vote again to decide if they want the same Senator or a new one.

(continued)

people don't know what he believes in, because enough people don't trust Alexander, and that's the reason they voted for Aaron instead of Alexander's father-in-law.

To Alexander, it feels like Aaron tried to beat Philip Schuyler for his spot in the Senate just to be mean, not because he actually cares about doing anything meaningful in Congress. Aaron insists he did it because he saw a chance to get what he wants, and that he was not trying to hurt Alexander or his family.[3]

(continued)

The House of Representatives is the part of Congress where each state gets a certain number of people to represent it depending on how many people live in that state. So, states with a lot of people have more representatives in Congress than states that don't have as many people. Representatives have their job for two years, unless the people vote to have them serve again.

To learn more about Congress, read the sidebar in "Farmer Refuted" (Song #6).

This is the point in Alexander and Aaron's lives when they really start to dislike each other.

---

1 The two main "parties," or groups, in American government during this time were the Federalists, which

Alexander was a leader of, and the **Democratic-Republicans**, which Thomas and James were the leaders of. Each party had different ideas about how the country should work.

2 Aaron didn't really change the party he was part of. He was basically always more of a Democratic-Republican than a Federalist. But since he was never very outspoken about his beliefs, the show makes it seem like he only decided to be a Democratic-Republican so he could try to become a Senator and get political power.

3 FUN FACT: After Aaron was a Senator for six years (one term), Eliza's father got his job back. This was one of the things that started making Aaron extra angry with Alexander, because he blamed Alexander for making people not like him or not vote for him.

30. CABINET BATTLE #2
Alexander and Thomas argue about whether or not to help France

It's another Cabinet meeting, and this time they are debating whether or not the United States should help France in a war it started with England and other countries in Europe. George wants to hear their ideas, but he reminds them he gets to make the final decision himself.

Thomas wants everyone to remember that France was a huge help to the colonies during the American Revolution. Without France's help, Britain probably would have won the war, so the United States owes a lot of thanks to France. He also reminds everyone the colonies did promise to help France someday if they needed it,[1] so it makes sense to help them now.[2]

Thomas finishes his argument by saying Alexander's ideas about this topic shouldn't really matter anyway, because it's not part of his job. Alexander is in charge of the money, not what the country does with other countries. After making his points, Thomas says a few mean things about Alexander before ending his argument.

When it's Alexander's turn to talk, he takes a dramatic pause and then angrily shouts at Thomas. He says Thomas is completely crazy if he thinks George is going to have the country be part of another war right after finishing its own war with Britain. He also argues that the promise the colonies made to France was with King Louis, who is not alive anymore.

George stops Alexander's sassy rant. He agrees with Alexander—the country is not strong enough right now to help other countries with their fights. He points out that there is a lot of craziness going on in France, and there isn't even a real leader there right now, so it's just not a good idea to get involved. He asks Alexander to write a statement declaring that the United States will not get involved or take sides in the war.[3]

George leaves, and Thomas and Alexander keep talking. Thomas says Alexander is not being a good friend to Lafayette by not helping France. Alexander says he knows Lafayette will be fine. He adds that if the United States tries to get involved in every revolution happening around the world, they will always be in a war somewhere. Thomas tries to insult Alexander a little bit, and then he ends the conversation by saying Alexander wouldn't be nearly as powerful or important if George didn't agree with him so much.

---

1 The promise was actually to help France protect their land in North America if they needed it, *not* to help France in a war across the ocean. Also, the United States promised to help if France was *attacked* by another country. But in this situation, France was pretty much the one who *started* the war with a lot of other countries.

2 In real life, Thomas actually agreed with the rest of the Cabinet, including Alexander, that the United States should stay out of France's war. What he did *not* agree with was making an official statement about it. One reason was he didn't really think the president was even *allowed* to do that. Because the Constitution only gives Congress the right to declare war, Thomas believed that meant the president did not have the power to declare *peace*.

3 This was called the Proclamation of Neutrality. **Neutral** means not helping either side in an argument. Jefferson asked for the statement to *not* include the word "neutrality" anywhere in it, and Washington allowed him to have it his way. They used the word "**impartial**" instead, which also means not taking sides.

31. WASHINGTON ON YOUR SIDE

Thomas wants to uncover something bad about Alexander

Aaron talks with Thomas and James about how nice it must be for Alexander to have George always agree with him.

Thomas blames Alexander for the fighting in the Cabinet and the fact that they have split up into separate groups with different beliefs now. He blames Alexander's money plan for making the farmers poor, and he doesn't like that the people who work with the money are the ones getting rich.

Thomas says he wants to find "dirt" on Alexander, which means he wants to find out some kind of bad secret Alexander might be hiding, or something bad he has done.[1]

James doesn't like that Alexander has made the **federal**, or whole-country, government so big and powerful. James and Thomas are both upset about Alexander's money plan putting the federal government in charge of all the money, instead of the states being in charge. They also think Alexander doesn't care about the South. They think he only cares about the North, which is where he lives, and the federal government.

Thomas feels like it's partly his fault for letting Alexander get so much power, since he is part of the Cabinet, too. He thinks he might have to quit being part of the Cabinet, because then he won't be connected to the things Alexander does anymore.

Thomas, James, and Aaron all complain again about Alexander being an immigrant. They think he doesn't belong in government and shouldn't have power because he was not born in America. They decide they are going to find out if he has been misusing any of the government money he is in charge of, or any of the special information about money he could have learned from being Treasury Secretary. By doing some detective work to find out where the money is going, they can find out if Alexander is getting extra money he shouldn't be getting.[2] **What do you think? Will they uncover anything?**

1 Thomas often asked other people to help him say or do mean things to people he didn't like. By having other people do those things, Thomas could pretend he was too respectable or too busy working on more important things to bother with childish name-calling or any nastiness.

2 At the end of their conversation, Thomas mentions something about the emperor having no clothes. This is from an imaginary story from a long time ago, about an **emperor**, who is kind of like a king. In the story, the emperor bought clothes he thought were magical. He was told they were only invisible to people who were not good enough at their jobs. Really, there were no clothes at all, but people were too afraid to say something to the powerful emperor. They didn't want him to think they were not good at their jobs, and they didn't want him to get mad at them. So they just stayed quiet.

When he refers to this story, Thomas is saying he, James, and Aaron are the only ones who are brave enough to tell the truth about Alexander being George's favorite. Thomas is also saying Alexander isn't as great as Alexander, George, and other people think he is, and he is not afraid to say so.

32. ONE LAST TIME
George tells Alexander he's done being president

George is in his office, and he has asked Alexander to come see him. When he arrives, George says he has a warning for him. Alexander is afraid he's getting in trouble for something, so he immediately blames whatever it is on Thomas. George says Thomas **resigned** earlier today,[1] which means he told George he is quitting his job as Secretary of State.

Alexander quickly comes up with lots of ways he can be mean to Thomas for quitting and upsetting George. He's so busy talking, he's not really listening or paying attention— George *isn't* upset. He tells Alexander not to talk so much, just like Aaron told him when they first met.

George explains that Thomas resigned because he wants to try to become the next president.[2] Alexander thinks that is hilarious, because he doesn't believe Thomas has any chance of beating George in an election. George adds that he has decided he's not going to **run** again for president— this is going to be his last time. Alexander is shocked!

> **Run for office:** When someone wants to try to get elected, or have people vote for them, they are "running for office," or "running for president" in this example.

George says he cannot be president forever, and he wants to show the American people that the United States will still be a great country, even with someone else being the president.[3] He asks Alexander to start writing his goodbye message. In the message, he wants to share some of the important things he's learned as president, and what he hopes for the future of the country, like how he doesn't think the United States should get involved in other countries' fights, and how he doesn't want the political parties to fight so much with each other.

George is really looking forward to just relaxing at home, and enjoying the wonderful country he helped create, without having to be in charge of military **troops** or big decisions. Alexander begs him to keep serving as president, but George has already made up his mind.

The two of them take turns saying some of the words Alexander writes for George's message.[4] They say even though George is not aware of any big mistakes he's made, he's sure he has probably made some. He hopes people will forgive him for those mistakes, and he also hopes they know how much he loves the United States. He tells them he's looking forward to being able to enjoy regular life in this incredible country with its great laws, ideas, beliefs, and freedom.[5]

George knows history is "watching" him—he knows that the way he says goodbye, and the choice he is making to end his presidency and let someone else become the next president peacefully, will be really important for many, many years. He knows his choices as the first president of the United States of America will be a model for future presidents to follow, so he wants to make sure he does a good job all the way to the end, including *how* his presidency ends.

---

1 Thomas actually resigned in 1793, more than two and a half years before George asked Alexander to help him write his farewell address in 1796.

2 Thomas said he was resigning because he just wanted to live a peaceful, quiet life at his home in Monticello, away from all of the arguing with Alexander and other people in government. But then he ran for president in 1796. He lost by just three votes, so he became John Adams' vice president. He ran for president again four years later in 1800.

3 George also did not want to try to be president for a third **term**, or time, because he really didn't want to die while he was still the president. He didn't want the American people to think anyone should stay president for the rest of their life. For almost 100 years, future presidents followed his example and did not run for president for a third term.

There was only one president, Franklin D. Roosevelt, who did serve more than two terms, from 1933 to 1945. After that, Congress made an **amendment**, or change, to the Constitution so no one could be elected, or chosen, to be president more than twice.

4 Most of the words in this part of the song are from George's actual Farewell Address, which was his "goodbye message" that was printed in newspapers all across the country. Alexander really did help George write the message, but George made the final decisions about what it said.

5 It is mentioned earlier in Song #20, "The Battle of Yorktown (The World Turned Upside Down)," but it's important to remember not everyone in the country was free at this time. There were still thousands and thousands of enslaved people who did not have any freedom at all.

33. I KNOW HIM

King George is very surprised about who the next president is

King George is shocked that George Washington decided to give up the power he had as president of the United States. He can't believe anyone would choose to just stop having that kind of power when they could keep it for a longer time. He also doesn't understand the idea of the people replacing who is in charge of the country by voting for a new leader—that's not how his country or most other countries work during this time.[1]

King George wonders who they could possibly choose as the next president. When he finds out it is going to be John Adams, he bursts out laughing. He remembers meeting John one time a few years ago, and he doesn't think he seems like someone who will be a very strong leader.

Like a lot of people in the United States and around the world, King George really doesn't think *anyone* can be as good a president as George Washington. He becomes giddy with delight[2] imagining how the American people will probably fight a lot with each other, how they won't respect or admire John the way they admired George, and how the whole country might just completely fall apart.

1 This is a little complicated, but Great Britain did have a leader whose job is called a prime minister, in addition to the King. This person is in charge of most of the government, but the King (or Queen) is the one who chooses the prime minister. Britain still has a prime minister (and a Queen) today.

2 When King George laughs hysterically and wishes America "good luck," he is being **sarcastic**. That means he's joking and doesn't really mean what he says. In this example, he's saying "good luck," but he doesn't actually think America has a chance of being successful with John as the president...and he's not really wishing them luck. He's kind of hoping it becomes one big mess for America.

34. THE ADAMS ADMINISTRATION
Alexander gets really mad at President John Adams for calling him names

Aaron gives a sneak-peek about what happens in the next few songs, when everything basically falls apart for Alexander. Aaron also quickly mentions a few of the things Alexander helped create, like the United States Coast Guard and the newspaper, *The New York Post.*

John Adams, the new president, has Thomas as his vice president.[1] Neither one of them like Alexander very much, even though John and Alexander are both leaders of the Federalist party.

John calls Alexander some mean names[2] and says nasty things about him, and Alexander gets really, really mad. He decides to write a **pamphlet**, just like he did when he was arguing with Samuel Seabury a long time ago. He writes a lot of very mean things about John in it.[3] Without George around to help Alexander calm down and think about his choices, his temper gets a little out of control.

James Madison is thrilled Alexander has made himself *and* the other main leader of the Federalists, John, both look really bad and crazy. He hopes that makes it so the Democratic-

Republicans will get to make more decisions and be more in charge now. But Thomas is not so sure. He believes Alexander might still cause problems for them, and he wants to make sure that doesn't happen. He says it's time for them to tell Alexander the bad, secret things they think they found out about him.

---

1 A long time ago, whoever got the second highest number of votes for president became vice president. Today, when someone runs for president, he or she decides ahead of time who the vice president will be if they win. So now when people vote, they make one vote for the pair they want—it's a vote for the president AND the vice president together.

2 The song says John fired Alexander from his job, but in real life Alexander quit being Secretary of the Treasury in 1795, two years before John became president. Even though he quit, he still had a lot of strong feelings and ideas about how the country should work. He also had a lot of power and friends in government. John *did* end up firing several people from his Cabinet when he found out they were taking advice from Alexander and listening to him more than they listened to John. He did not like that at all.

3 Alexander actually wanted what he wrote about John

to stay private and only be shared within the Federalist party—he didn't mean for it to be printed in the newspapers for everyone to read. But Aaron found it and had it published, which ended up being very embarrassing for Alexander (and for John).

35. WE KNOW

Thomas, James, and Aaron learn about Alexander's secret

Alexander is surprised to get a visit from Thomas, James, and Aaron.[1] They claim they have proof Alexander used the power and information he had as the leader of the United States Treasury Department to make extra money illegally. What they call their proof is a record of Alexander making separate payments adding up to almost a thousand dollars[2] to James Reynolds a few years ago, a man who they know did illegal things. They tell Alexander he's in big trouble, and they say he's never going to be able to work in government again.[3]

Alexander knows he didn't do anything illegal, but he wants to prove it to them. He asks the three men to promise not to tell anyone what he's going to show them, and they say okay—even though they sound like they might not really mean it. He shows them the first letter James Reynolds sent him, when he found out about Alexander and Maria's affair and told Alexander he had to give James money if he wanted him to keep it a secret. Alexander explains to the men that he did pay James a lot of money not to tell anyone.

Alexander basically says, "See? I told you I didn't do anything against the law. Even though I made a really bad choice to visit Maria a lot of times, I didn't do anything wrong with the government's money—it was all my own money."

Thomas, James, and Aaron are shocked about what Alexander just told them—it wasn't what they were expecting to find out. They believe his explanation for why he paid James Reynolds,[4] and they don't think he did anything illegal with the Treasury's money. They agree not to tell anyone about it. But Aaron warns Alexander about **rumors**, which are stories people hear that might or might not be true. He says rumors tend to get bigger and keep spreading, so more and more people hear about them. This makes Alexander not so sure Aaron will keep the secret.

1 In real life, it was actually Senator James Monroe (who later became the fifth president of the United States) and two other members of Congress who visited Alexander. James Reynolds, Maria's husband, was in jail and told them Alexander had been doing illegal things with the country's money. So they visited Alexander to ask him about it. He told them about his affair with Maria, and he strongly denied doing anything wrong with the country's money. He gave them copies of the letters Maria and James had sent him, as proof.

The three men seemed to believe him and agreed to keep it a secret, but guess who James Monroe sent the copies of the letters to? Thomas Jefferson! Well, at least that's what most people think James Monroe meant when he told Alexander the original papers were "in the hands of a respectable character in Virginia."

2 Alexander paid James Reynolds $1,000 the first time, and then he paid him about $100 more during the next few months after that. That would be more than $20,000 in today's money!

3 When the three men visited Alexander to ask him about this situation, they said they wanted to give him a chance to explain. They weren't sure whether James Reynolds had told them the truth or was lying.

4 James Monroe later wrote that he wasn't sure if Alexander's explanation was true. Alexander asked him many times to say he believed him, but James would not do it. (The other two men did.) Alexander and James almost dueled because of this, but Aaron Burr helped stop it.

There has never been any proof Alexander took money from the Treasury to make extra money for himself.

36. HURRICANE

Alexander decides he has to take charge of what happens next

Alexander is thinking about the conversation he just had with Thomas, James, and Aaron, and he is feeling nervous. As he thinks out loud to himself, he says the middle of a hurricane—a part of the storm called the "eye"—is very calm and quiet, even though just outside the eye it is incredibly dangerous.

That is how Alexander feels about this moment right now: it is calm and quiet. But he senses that bad things might happen soon, now that a few people—especially people who don't like him very much—know his secret about Maria. In his mind, it feels like there is a scary storm out there, just waiting to tear his life apart.

Note: Calling Alexander's situation a hurricane is a **metaphor**. That is when one thing is called something else that feels, acts, looks, or seems kind of the same as the first thing. So, instead of saying a crazy situation "*feels like* a hurricane," someone might say "It *is* a hurricane." Metaphors help other people imagine what the situation is like.

Alexander remembers how, when he was 17, an actual hurricane destroyed his entire town. Somehow, he survived.

He wrote a letter to his father describing what had happened and how horrible it was. His letter got published in the local newspaper. Many people were so impressed with his writing that they donated money to help send Alexander to New York. He believes his ability to write well was what saved him.

Alexander thinks back on countless other times his writing helped him, like when it helped him be part of the war, and made Eliza fall in love with him, and helped people understand why the Constitution was so great, and explained how the country's money would work.[1] In the past, his writing has saved him and helped him create amazing things, so he decides that writing is the very best thing for him to do in this situation. He can tell his story his own way, before someone else has a chance to tell it for him.[2]

Before he starts writing, he remembers back to when he and his mother both were very sick. She held him in her arms as she was dying.[3] Even though he was also very sick, Alexander didn't die. He got better and survived.

Alexander is alone, thinking about these memories of really hard moments in his life. He is getting ready to write about what he and Maria did, so he can prove he did not do anything wrong with the country's money. Just as he decides to do this, Aaron and the **ensemble**, or group of people on stage, start to chant "Wait," over and over. This could be for a lot of different reasons. They might be telling Alexander, "Wait, don't do it! Don't tell everyone this secret!" Or it could be Aaron saying, "You don't think you can die? Just wait, it will happen soon." Or Aaron could be saying to himself, or to the audience, "I'm gonna wait to see the mess Alexander makes of this whole thing." It could even be a voice in Alexander's head, wondering what Aaron would do if he was in this situation. **What do you think it means?**

Eliza, Angelica, Maria, and George all come together on the side, like voices in Alexander's mind trying to remind him that what he is about to do will have an impact on his life and how he will be remembered. And if he puts it all in writing, there will be a record of it forever.

But, if Alexander hears these voices in his mind, begging

him to think again about what he is planning to do, he doesn't listen to them. He has already made his decision to write about what he did with Maria and tell the whole world about it. He believes this is the only way to protect his reputation and prove he didn't do anything illegal with the country's money. He writes something called the "Reynolds Pamphlet."

---

1 Alexander wrote the country's debt plan that ended up creating the national debt, by taking all of the states' debts and combining them. He also created the national bank, and he helped create the U.S. Mint, which is where coins are made.

2 What really happened is a man named James Callender found out about the letters between Alexander and James Reynolds. He published a few pamphlets accusing Alexander of doing illegal things as the Secretary of the Treasury, and also of having an affair with Maria. So, people already knew the **rumors** about Maria and about the bad things Alexander was accused of doing in his job as Treasury Secretary.

3 We don't know if Alexander's mom was holding him, but since they were both so ill the two of them were separated from the rest of the family in a room together. Even if she was not holding him in her arms, they were very close to each other when she died.

37. THE REYNOLDS PAMPHLET
Alexander writes about his secret, and everyone is shocked

Everybody is talking about the Reynolds Pamphlet[1] Alexander wrote describing his relationship with Maria Reynolds.[2] Aaron, Thomas, and James read it aloud together.

In the pamphlet, Alexander writes that people are accusing him of doing things he shouldn't have done with the country's money—things that were illegal. He explains he didn't do anything like that at all, but he *did* kiss Maria Reynolds. A lot. And her husband knew about it and said it was ok. He says Eliza and the children were away most of the time, staying at her father's house.[3]

Everyone is really surprised by what Alexander did. And they are also incredibly shocked by all of the personal details he shares with the whole world in the pamphlet. They all say, over and over, there is no way he will ever become president, now that he has admitted to making such terrible choices and not being such a great person. Thomas is shocked, too, but he is also happy his wish for Alexander to never be the president looks like it is probably going to come true.

Angelica arrives from London,[4] and Alexander thinks she

has come to help him get through the mess he's made. He is sure she is on his side and will understand why he wrote the pamphlet. Angelica quickly tells Alexander she did not come for him. She's here to help Eliza. Angelica knows her sister loves Alexander so much, and that she will be heartbroken about what Alexander has done—especially because he wrote about it and shared it with the entire world. Angelica is incredibly disappointed in Alexander for not being satisfied with having Eliza as his wife.

♪ Musical Note: Right before Angelica arrives, part of the music from "Satisfied" can quietly be heard. It's quiet, making us not very sure how she is going to react to what Alexander has done. As she continues talking, the "Satisfied" music gets stronger, showing Angelica's strong feelings (of anger) about what he did.

In the middle of everyone talking about how they cannot believe what Alexander has done, he shouts out, "At least I didn't do anything wrong with the country's money!" That was the whole reason he wrote the pamphlet—to prove his innocence as Treasury Secretary. He wanted to prove he gave James Reynolds his *own* money to stop him from telling anyone about his relationship with Maria. Was it worth it? Everyone else thinks he has ruined his life with this choice.

At the very end, people say they feel really sorry for Eliza. They know her feelings must be deeply hurt because of what happened—Alexander having a relationship with Maria *and* the fact that he let everyone know about it with his pamphlet.

1 The pamphlet Alexander wrote was actually titled "Observations on Certain Documents Contained in No. V & VI of 'The History of the United States for the Year 1796,' In Which the Charge of Speculation Against Alexander Hamilton, Late Secretary of the Treasury, Is Fully Refuted. Written by Himself." It became known as the "Reynolds Pamphlet," which is a much shorter name!

2 The Reynolds Pamphlet was 37 pages long, *plus* 58 pages of additional documents. The extra documents were mostly copies of letters to Alexander from James and Maria, and letters between Alexander and the three men from Congress who were the first to find out about the whole thing.

Alexander's close friends believed he could have just written one or two paragraphs to prove his innocence. Everyone was very surprised at how incredibly long his response to James Callender's accusations turned out to be. (See Song #36, footnote #2, for more information about what made Alexander want to write about the affair.)

3 A lot of the words in this song are the actual words Alexander wrote in his pamphlet. In it, he also says he knows it will really hurt Eliza's feelings that he is telling everyone what he did. But he says he thinks she will agree with his choice to write about it, so he can prove he didn't do anything wrong with the country's money.

We don't know for sure how Eliza felt about Alexander's choice to write the Reynolds Pamphlet, but she is definitely NOT happy about it in this story.

4 Angelica and her husband had already moved back to the United States a few months before Alexander published the Reynolds Pamphlet.

38. BURN
Eliza reacts, alone

Eliza is alone. She is holding a stack of letters in her hand, along with a lantern. She is thinking out loud to herself, and she speaks softly at first. She is thinking about the many letters Alexander wrote to her, especially the ones from when they were first falling in love.

Eliza says she used to know for sure that Alexander only loved her, that his heart belonged to her. But now she knows that is not true anymore, and she is trying to figure out how this could have happened. She remembers Angelica warning her in the beginning that Alexander would do whatever the best thing was for *him*, even if it might hurt other people. It feels like that is exactly what is happening now.

As Eliza thinks back, she remembers how powerful Alexander's letters to her were. His words made her feel so special and made her fall completely in love with him. She doesn't understand how he could hurt her like this now, when he seemed to love her so much. She thinks about how, when they first fell in love, it felt like the world was on fire. Maybe it was because the love she felt for him was so strong, it seemed like her heart was burning with passion. Maybe it was because it felt like the whole world had burned away and disappeared, and only the two of them were left, so in love.

Eliza is **devastated**, which means very heartbroken and incredibly sad, that Alexander published the letters Maria wrote to him, claiming she loved him and couldn't wait to see him again. It hurts Eliza's heart that Alexander didn't think about how his wife would feel when everyone found out about his relationship with Maria. She can't believe it was more important to Alexander to prove he didn't do anything wrong with the country's money, than it was to think about Eliza and how hurt and embarrassed she would feel if he told everyone about Maria. He made his **reputation**, or what other people think about him, more important than his own wife's feelings.[1]

Eliza says that when Angelica learned what Alexander had done, she told Eliza he is like Icarus, a young man in a made-up story from a long, long, long time ago. In the story, Icarus' father gave him wings to fly, and Icarus became so excited with his new special power that he flew too close to the sun, which melted the wax holding the feathers together. Because of this, Icarus fell into the ocean and did not survive.

Eliza sees how this same kind of thing has happened to Alexander. His **ambition**—his desire to do great things, to "rise up" and build a legacy—is what has now caused his failure. He was so focused on his own greatness and reputation that he didn't consider the bad things that could happen. He may have protected his reputation as Treasury Secretary, but he destroyed his marriage and any chance he could have had of "flying" higher and becoming president.

Eliza decides to burn all of her letters to Alexander, so no one in the future will ever know how hurt she was when all of this happened. Alexander has destroyed their love and anything special they shared together, and it breaks her heart. She doesn't want anyone to know how much pain she is feeling,[2] and she doesn't want people to know about the good she used to see in him. She fiercely declares that Alexander doesn't get to have her heart, or her love, anymore. The only thing he will get to keep is his memory of how much she used to love him. She is hurting deeply, and she says she hopes he feels as much pain and suffering as she does right now.

1 Some of the newspapers wrote really nasty things about Eliza when this happened, insulting her for choosing to marry a man who would have a romantic relationship with another woman. So, in addition to hurting Eliza's feelings, Alexander also hurt her reputation.

2 We don't know when or how Eliza found out about Alexander and Maria. We also don't know how Eliza reacted when she found out about it, or what she did or felt when he told the whole world about it by writing a 95-page pamphlet.

39. BLOW US ALL AWAY
Philip gets into a big argument about his father

♪ **Musical Note:** A lot of the words Philip says in the beginning of this song are exactly the same or very close to the words Alexander says in Song #3, "My Shot."

It's a few years later, and Alexander and Eliza's son Philip is all grown up. He recently graduated from the same college his father went to, and he is proud that people say he's a lot like his father in many different ways. But he wants to be "**bolder**," which means being even braver and doing even bigger things than his father has done. He remembers how his father used to tell him someday Philip would blow everyone away, or really amaze everyone.

Philip is walking down the street and asks two young ladies he meets if they know where George Eacker is. He says George made a speech last week and said some mean things about his father, Alexander.[1] Philip is upset about it and wants George to apologize. The ladies tell him George is watching a play.

129

♪ Musical Note: The scratchy sound of a music record moving back and forth is also used in "Ten Duel Commandments." It gives the listener a clue that a duel is coming.

Philip goes to the theater and walks up to George in the middle of the show. He says George shouldn't have said the mean things he did about his father. George refuses to apologize, because he believes everything he said was true. To defend his father's honor and reputation, Philip challenges George to a duel.[2] George says he's going to finish watching the play, and they can have the duel later.[3]

Philip talks to his father to get advice on what to do in a duel. Alexander asks if Philip and George's friends, or **seconds**, tried to solve the disagreement by talking about it first. Philip explains that George would not apologize for what he said, so they were done trying to talk it out.[4]

Alexander tells Philip to go to the duel, and stand up tall and brave. He says when Philip and George are facing each other for the duel, Philip should shoot his gun straight up into the sky, instead of at George. He says George will do the same thing if he is an honorable man. Alexander reminds Philip you can't take back ending someone's life. If you do that, it is something you will live with forever.

Alexander asks Philip to promise he won't shoot George. He knows it would break Eliza's heart if her son killed someone, and her heart is already hurting so much because of what Alexander has done. Philip promises.

Philip sings a different version of the song he sang for his dad on his ninth birthday. He starts by admitting he's a little bit nervous about dueling. He talks about how proud he is of his father, and how he feels like he has to make George realize it's not okay to say mean things about him. **What do you think? Is there something else Philip could do instead of having a duel? What would you do?**

Philip and George arrive at the place where they are going to duel. Philip asks him how the play was, but George doesn't want to chat, he just wants to get the duel started. Philip reminds everyone there that the duel will happen after they finish counting to ten. Those are the rules everyone knows, but he's just reminding everybody.

The counting starts. When they get to seven, there is a gunshot! What happened? George did not follow the rules, and he didn't aim for the sky like Philip was planning to do. Instead, he shot Philip.[5]

---

1 George Eacker gave his speech in front of people at a Fourth of July celebration. Afterwards, his speech was published in the newspapers, which is how Philip found out about it. Philip actually didn't see George until more than four months after his speech, not one week later.

Also, we don't know for sure if George actually said anything mean about Alexander in his speech. Most people at the time said he did not, but some people claimed he said Alexander did not think it would be a bad thing for people to physically force Thomas Jefferson to stop being the president.

2 George was very embarrassed by the scene Philip and his friend, Stephen Price, caused at the theater when they started yelling at him and being rude. He called them "rascals," which was considered an insult. And *that* is why Philip *and* his friend Stephen Price both challenged George to a duel.

3 Read about Song #15, "The Ten Duel Commandments," to learn more about duels.

4 Even though Alexander did give Philip this advice about the duel, he did *not* know when the **negotiations**, or discussions, had ended. He didn't find out until the morning of the duel, when it was too late.

5 In the actual duel, this is not how it happened. They did count to ten. Then, George and Philip both just stood there and stared at each other for about one minute. Neither of them raised their gun. Then George raised his gun, and so did Philip. George shot Philip above his right hip.

In George's duel with Stephen the day before, the two men went through three or four rounds, or turns, of shooting before they decided to end the duel. They shook hands and made up.

40. STAY ALIVE (REPRISE)
Alexander and Eliza are really worried about Philip

Alexander rushes in to the doctor's house[1] to see Philip. He heard that Philip was shot in the duel. He is terrified, but he is hoping Philip will live. The doctor[2] explains Philip has lost a lot of blood and his wound is infected.

When Alexander goes into the room where Philip is lying on the doctor's table, he sees Philip is hurt really, really badly and in a lot of pain.[3] Philip tells his father he did exactly what Alexander had told him to do. Alexander says he knows, and he tries to comfort Philip and asks him to rest. He wants Philip to save all the energy he has in order to stay alive. Alexander also feels very guilty, thinking it's his fault for telling Philip what to do in the duel and to go to the duel at all. He feels especially guilty since the reason Philip even had the duel was because he was defending Alexander against the mean things George Eacker had said about him.

♪ Musical Note: The way Alexander (and Eliza later) repeats the words "I know" sounds a lot like a heartbeat. It is a symbol for how they are trying to do anything they can to help Philip stay alive.

Eliza rushes into the room, overcome with fear for her son's life. She is incredibly scared for Philip and hopes with all her heart that he will live. She asks Alexander if he knows who hurt Philip, and if he knew about the duel ahead of time. Alexander had not told her about the duel, because he thought it would be better if she didn't know about it. But now they are both **devastated** as they see their son in pain and know he might not survive.

Philip apologizes to his mother for not remembering what she taught him. He might be talking about forgetting to keep something that was important to her in his mind—maybe she thinks dueling is wrong for people to do. Or maybe he realizes it was a bad choice to get so upset about what someone else says about his father. **What lesson from his mom do you think he might be sorry for forgetting?**

Philip and Eliza talk about how they used to play piano together. They are happy thinking back on these special memories. They smile, remembering how Philip always changed the way the words were sung when he practiced counting in French. Then, the same way Alexander did, Eliza tells Philip to stop talking for now. She wants to keep talking with him, but she knows he needs to rest.

As Philip and Eliza begin to count to nine in French together, with his mother and father at his side, Philip stops breathing. He is gone.[4]

---

1 Philip was actually taken to Angelica's house after the duel. When Alexander heard Philip and George had already stopped trying to work out their disagreement and were planning to duel, he rushed to Dr. Hosack's house to ask him for help. The doctor's family told him Dr. Hosack had already left that morning to go to the duel with Philip.

When Alexander heard this, he was so overwhelmed with fear for Philip's life that he **fainted**, which means his brain suddenly went to sleep and he fell down.

When he woke up a few hours later, he went to Angelica's house right away to see Philip.

2 This same doctor had already saved Philip's life four years earlier, when he was very sick from a really bad fever.

Fun Fact: The actor who plays the doctor in the show also plays Philip Schuyler *and* James Reynolds!

3 When Alexander saw how hurt Philip was and how pale his face was, he turned away, grabbed the doctor's hand, and cried, "Doctor, I despair!" **Despair** means having absolutely no hope. Alexander was sure Philip was not going to survive.

4 Eliza was pregnant when Philip died. When the new baby was born, she and Alexander decided to name him Philip after the son they had lost.

41. IT'S QUIET UPTOWN
Alexander and Eliza grieve the heartbreaking loss of their son

Angelica sadly and softly explains that sometimes there are no words to describe how much pain and sadness people are feeling. And sometimes they are suffering so much, there are no words to help them. Losing a child creates a pain in a parent's heart that is so strong, people can't imagine what it feels like unless they have experienced it themselves. Alexander and Eliza are heartbroken and speechless, so Angelica tells this part of the story for them.

After losing Philip, Alexander and Eliza move to a different part of town, called uptown[1]. It's a lot quieter there than it was downtown, and Alexander has a lot of time to think to himself. He works in his garden, and he goes to church. He walks around town, sometimes talking to himself, sometimes imagining he is talking to Philip, who isn't really there. Alexander misses Philip so much, and he is so sorry for hurting Eliza's heart. To Alexander, it feels like his whole life has fallen into a thousand pieces all around him, and he's just trying to make it through each day, one at a time.

Alexander tells Eliza he wishes more than anything that he could bring Philip back, even if it means Alexander would have to trade places with Philip and be the one who died instead. He tells Eliza he knows she may not be ready to forgive him for what he did with Maria, or for writing the Reynolds Pamphlet, or for knowing about Philip's duel and not telling her or stopping it. He admits he has no idea how hard it will be for them to get through this tragedy, and he doesn't know what he should do. He asks if she will please just let him stand next to her, because that is the only thing that matters to him now.

Alexander walks alongside Eliza, trying very hard to earn her forgiveness and get her to let him back into her life. Angelica continues telling the story. She says again that there are some moments words just cannot describe. This time, though, she says sometimes it is **grace**, or kindness and forgiveness, rather than pain and suffering, that is so powerful it cannot be explained in words. As they stand in the garden together, Eliza reaches over and takes Alexander's hand, offering him forgiveness.[2]

Now, hand in hand, they walk together. They are still heartbroken and grieving the loss of their beloved son, but now they can try to help each other get through this unimaginable time.

---

1 The Hamiltons' new home, The Grange, was finished in 1802. Alexander had already started planning it three years before Philip's death. It was named after Alexander's father's family's home in Scotland. The house was moved a few times over the years, just a few blocks away each time. Now it is back on the original land where Alexander first had it built, in the Harlem neighborhood of Upper Manhattan, New York.

2 In the show, when Eliza is willing to forgive Alexander and let him back into her life, it is a very powerful and emotional moment. He bursts into tears, because he is so thankful he hasn't lost Eliza forever. He is grateful they can try to grieve together, and maybe, just maybe, they can get back some of their love and trust that he destroyed.

42. THE ELECTION OF 1800
Aaron and Thomas are both trying to become the next president

It's 1800[1] now, and people are getting ready to vote for who they want the next president to be. According to Thomas, people are not very happy with John Adams as the president, and Alexander isn't really involved in politics right now[2]. In this election, Thomas and Aaron are both trying to become the next president.[3]

James tells Thomas it's possible for Aaron to win, even though people don't even really know what he believes in.[4] James says maybe Thomas should try to get Alexander to convince people to vote for Thomas. It's a bit of a strange idea to suggest, since Thomas and Alexander don't like each other and don't agree on almost anything when it comes to politics.

Aaron is walking around town asking people to vote for him. A lot of the people in the Federalist party aren't sure who they want to vote for, so they ask Alexander who he thinks should be president—Thomas or Aaron? Alexander has been enjoying the quiet time he has had uptown, where he is a little bit further away from everything happening in politics. He runs into Aaron, who admits it is a lot of work walking around and talking to people, but he's happy to be going after what he wants. Aaron says that is something he learned from Alexander.

When the election happens, it ends up in a *tie!* Now the House of Representatives (part of Congress) has to decide who will be president: Thomas or Aaron.[5] Alexander speaks up and says even though they have never agreed on anything,[6] he thinks Thomas should be the president. He explains that at least Thomas has beliefs and tells people what those beliefs are—Aaron does not. Thomas and James are very surprised Alexander gave his support to Thomas and helped him win.

Aaron congratulates Thomas on winning. He adds that he is looking forward to being Thomas' partner, since the rules say whoever gets second place becomes the vice president. Thomas is not happy about that—he does not trust Aaron at all. He tells James he is going to change that rule, since he's the president now.[7]

---

1 In real life, Philip died in November 1801, a whole year after this election.

2 In the way the story is told in the show, this feels like Alexander is not around because he is grieving Philip's death and lives away from the action and politics in the city. In real life, Alexander was in charge of the United States Army during this time, and he was busy getting the troops ready for a war they thought might happen with France.

3 In "Hamilton," the story makes it seem like Thomas and Aaron are both trying to become president. Really, Thomas was the one **running for**, or trying to become, president. Aaron was running as his vice president, at least in the beginning. (See footnote #5 for what happened next.)

   Fun fact: Aaron tried to become president four years earlier, in 1796, but he came in fourth place.

4 Aaron Burr actually was outspoken about his beliefs and what he thought was right. He said he wanted to end slavery and free everyone who was enslaved (even though he personally enslaved people), he stood up for women's rights and thought they should be able to vote, and he believed girls should get the same education as boys.

   Aaron did want power, and he did work with people from both parties, which is why some people who didn't like him didn't feel they could trust him and weren't sure what he really wanted.

5 When the election happened, it didn't go quite as planned. Thomas and Aaron each got 73 votes, which made them tied for first place. So the House of Representatives had to vote to decide which one of them would be president and which one would be vice president.

The representatives took about a week, and they all voted over and over again—36 times! Either Thomas or Aaron had to have at least nine of the 16 states vote for them in order to win. Each time, neither one of them had enough votes to win. Finally, on the 36th vote, Thomas got 10 votes and became the president.

Part of the reason some representatives changed their vote was because Alexander begged his Federalist friends *not* to vote for Aaron. He felt that even though he and the other Federalists didn't agree with Thomas' ideas, Thomas was still a better choice than Aaron. Alexander said Aaron didn't believe in anything and couldn't be trusted. This is another reason Aaron became very angry at Alexander.

6 Alexander and Thomas actually did agree on some issues when they were in George's Cabinet.

7 The rule did get changed in 1804, with the 12th Amendment to the US Constitution.

43. YOUR OBEDIENT SERVANT
Aaron and Alexander write letters telling each other why they are upset

Aaron is *very* upset with Alexander. He can't begin to understand why Alexander would support Thomas, someone he has disliked from the moment he met him, just to stop Aaron from winning the election. Aaron wants so badly to have power and to be a part of making important political decisions. And even though he will get to be vice president now, Thomas doesn't trust him at all. So, he kind of got something he wanted by getting a special **title**, or job name, but it isn't turning out the way he thought it would. He's still not in charge and Thomas won't let him have any power.[1]

The way Aaron sees how things have happened, every time he has tried to get power, Alexander has stopped him from getting it, usually by saying mean things about him to other people.[2] It's true, Alexander *did* tell people not to vote for Aaron because he believes Aaron can't be trusted and only cares about himself. **But does that make it all Alexander's fault that Aaron hasn't gotten what he wants? Or is Alexander just sharing his opinion?**

Their conversation, through letters, goes like this:

Aaron is tired of Alexander being mean to him, so he writes him a letter. He says if Alexander is going to call him names, he should tell Aaron when and where they can duel. Aaron signs his letter "A. Burr" and sends it off to Alexander.

Alexander writes back to Aaron and says it's not his fault no one trusts Aaron. He says Aaron needs to be more specific about what exactly Alexander said to make him so upset to demand an apology. He sends back a list of all the things he's disagreed with Aaron about over the past 30 years, and he signs his letter "A. Ham." [3]

Aaron can't believe how obnoxious Alexander is being.

Alexander writes another letter, explaining that all he's ever done is try to do what's best for the country—which includes stopping Aaron from becoming president. Alexander says he does not want to duel, but he will not apologize for doing what he believes is right.[4]

Now Aaron is furious, because Alexander is refusing to apologize for the mean things he has said about Aaron. He says if Alexander doesn't apologize immediately, Aaron will challenge him to a duel.

Alexander still refuses to apologize. He says whatever he said about Aaron, he meant it and won't apologize for it. Alexander adds another insult, saying again that he believes Aaron only cares about himself.

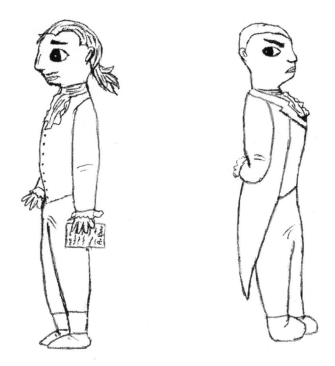

Because Alexander won't apologize and Aaron won't let it go because his reputation has been damaged, their letters back and forth end with the two of them agreeing to a duel at Weehawken, New Jersey.

---

1 Thomas and Aaron started out running together to be president and vice president. But when they each got 73 votes and tied, Aaron told people he would be happy if he was chosen to become president instead of vice president.

This is what made Thomas not trust Aaron at all, because when they first tied, Aaron said of course Thomas should get to be the president, not Aaron. That was their plan from the beginning. But when Aaron realized the electors might pick him instead, just to be mean to Thomas, he was pretty excited about having the chance to be president.

2 It wasn't actually the election of 1800 that finally made Aaron so mad he demanded that Alexander either apologize or duel. It was four years later, in April 1804, when Aaron ran for **governor** of New York. Before the election, the newspapers printed nasty things about him and about the man who won.

Two months later, in June, Aaron found out about something very insulting someone claimed Alexander had said about Aaron. And *that* is what made him so mad and offended that he wrote to Alexander, demanding an apology.

3 This is pretty much how these letters between Alexander and Aaron were in real life, except: there were only four letters delivered (not six), Alexander didn't really send a list of disagreements, and he signed his name "A. Hamilton," not "A. Ham." They both really did sign their names, "I have the honor to be your obedient servant," because that was a polite way of signing a letter back then.

The letter that got Aaron so upset in the first place claimed Alexander had shared an even "more despicable opinion" about Aaron besides calling him a "dangerous man" who can't be trusted. Aaron was understandably very offended by this.

Alexander was kind of tricky in his letter back to Aaron, basically saying, "How am I supposed to know what I might have said that someone else would think is more despicable than that? Or how can I know what you think might be so offensive that I would have to apologize for it?"

4 Alexander did *not* want this disagreement to end in a duel, but he knew it might. Before the actual duel, he wrote a note and put it away with his **will**, which is an important document that says where you want your money and belongings to go after you aren't alive anymore.

The note explained Alexander's thoughts about the duel, in case he did not survive. He wrote, "I am certainly desirous of avoiding this (duel)..." He says that when he replied to Aaron's letters, "I wished, as far as might be practicable, to leave a door open to **accommodation**," which means a compromise. But Alexander still refused to apologize, which would have stopped the duel from happening at all. He believed what he said was true and did not require an apology, so he was also being a bit stubborn about it.

44. BEST OF WIVES AND BEST OF WOMEN

Alexander tells Eliza he has a meeting and needs to finish writing something first

♪ **Musical Note:** The first few notes, or sounds, in this song are the same as the last few notes in Eliza's song, "That Would Be Enough" (Song #17) and the first few notes in "It's Quiet Uptown" (Song #41).

It's really late at night, or really early in the morning—sometime before the sun comes up. Alexander is writing at his desk. Eliza wakes up and asks him to come back to sleep. He tells her he has an early meeting and has to finish writing something important first.[1]

Eliza still doesn't understand why Alexander is *always* writing. She asks him again to come back to bed, and Alexander tells her he will be back from his meeting before she even wakes up again. Eliza asks him one more time to come back to sleep, and he says he has to go to his meeting soon, because it's happening before **dawn**, which is before the sun even comes up.

Eliza gives up and says she's going back to sleep. Alexander lovingly gives her hand a kiss and says she is the best wife and the best woman. [2] She goes back to bed.

———————————

1 Alexander wrote a note, called "Statement on Impending Duel with Aaron Burr," as well as two secret letters to Eliza, before the duel. These notes, his **will**, and a few other notes were all given to his friend Nathaniel Pendleton, who was his "second" in the duel with Aaron. Alexander asked Nathaniel to deliver them if he died in the duel.

2 In the first of his two secret letters to Eliza before the duel, Alexander did sign it, "Adieu best of wives and best of Women. Embrace all my darling Children for me. Ever yours, AH."

45. THE WORLD WAS WIDE ENOUGH

Alexander and Aaron duel, and Aaron regrets his decision

Aaron explains ten things about the duel before it starts.

1 Alexander and Aaron went across the river, in two separate boats, to the dueling place. Aaron and his friend, William P. Van Ness were in one boat, and...

2 ...Alexander, Alexander's friend Nathaniel Pendleton, and a doctor were in the other boat.

3 Aaron says when they got there, Alexander inspected the dueling area very closely. All Aaron could think about was how angry he was at Alexander for ruining all of the times he tried to get political power.[1]

4 They sort of "drew straws" to decide who would choose where he wanted to stand. Alexander won, and he seemed to be working extra hard to try to figure out which spot was the best.[2] Aaron thinks of Alexander as someone who has excellent **aim**, which means he is really good at shooting exactly where he wants.

5 Aaron didn't know it when he was there, but he found out later that the duel happened to be in the same place where Philip's duel had been.[3]

6 Aaron watched Alexander inspect his gun very closely before the duel. That made him nervous, and he started to think Alexander was definitely going to try to hurt him.

7 Aaron admits he is not very good at shooting a gun, especially compared to Alexander.[4]

8 Aaron noticed Alexander was wearing his glasses. He assumed it must be because he wanted to make sure he would hit Aaron when it was time to shoot. **What are some other reasons Alexander might have wanted to wear his glasses at the duel?**

With all of these things piling up in his mind, Aaron thinks, "Only one of us is going to survive this." He is certain Alexander is going to try to shoot him, and he doesn't want to be the one who dies. He says the most important thing to him is not having his daughter end up without any parents, which is what would happen if he died.[5]

9 When it's time for the duel, Alexander and Aaron look each other in the eye and get all of the courage they have.

10 Finally, they count to ten and take their paces. Aaron fires a shot at Alexander.[6]

♪ **Musical Note:** The music stops completely as Alexander starts thinking to himself. Lin-Manuel Miranda said this part of the show was one of the hardest parts for him to figure out. Then he realized *silence* was something he had not used yet, and he thought it was the perfect way to tell this part of the story.

Everything starts to go in really slow motion, where it's almost like time is stopping. Alexander has a lot of thoughts going quickly through his mind at this moment, and we get to hear what he is thinking. He has thought about dying so many times, and he wonders if this is when he will finally, actually die. He wonders what he should do. Should he shoot back, or do nothing? He thinks about how Aaron was his first friend when he arrived in America, and now they have become enemies. He wonders if Aaron's face will be the very last thing he sees before he dies.

Alexander thinks about his **legacy** and wonders how people will remember him after he dies. He is grateful for this country and proud he got to play such a special part in creating it.

Some people say that right before they die, they get a quick look at heaven. Alexander sees or imagines seeing his friend John Laurens, his son Philip, his mother, and George Washington,[7] all waiting for him in heaven. Then he thinks about Eliza, and he doesn't want to leave her. He hopes she will live for many more years, and he believes he will get to see her in heaven when she does die someday.

All of these thoughts race through Alexander's mind in less than one second.

At last, he decides what he is going to do. In his mind, he sings a line from the song he and his friends sang all those years ago when they first met. Then, he raises his arm up to the sky and shoots his gun into the air. Aaron yells, "Wait!"

But it is too late. Aaron has already shot Alexander. He tries to walk over to Alexander, but the others stop him.[8]

Alexander is rowed back home on the boat, dying.[9] Aaron goes out to get a drink. People everywhere are sobbing. They are so shocked and upset about what has happened and so furious with Aaron for what he has done. Aaron says Angelica and Eliza were both with Alexander when he died.

Aaron thinks about how death happens to good people and bad people—anyone can die. He also thinks about how now he will always be remembered for the mistakes he made—including killing Alexander. He realizes that when Alexander decided not to shoot at Aaron, he was the first of the two of them to die, but Aaron suffered the rest of his life for it. Lots of people hated Aaron for what he did, and he lost any chance of people liking him or letting him have any power, ever again. That's a really big price he had to "pay," or give up, that he did not think about ahead of time.

Aaron started the duel because he wanted to defend his honor and his reputation, but the duel is actually what ended up making him lose any chance of ever getting people to respect or like him again.[10]

Aaron wishes he would have realized he and Alexander could have both gone on living—that they didn't have to duel, that he could have just let Alexander's insults go. He wishes he would have realized ahead of time that Alexander being gone wouldn't make his life any better. But Alexander *is* gone now, and Aaron cannot ever change that or take it back.

Most people will only remember Aaron for this one thing—for killing Alexander Hamilton in a duel. How will they remember Alexander? What will his legacy be?

---

1 In real life, it wasn't the end of the election of 1800 that made Aaron the angriest at Alexander. It was later, in 1804, when Aaron tried to become **governor** of New York—the person in charge of the state. Alexander again used his influence to convince people not to vote for Aaron, so he lost. (See Song #43, footnotes 2 and 3 for more details.)

2 It may seem like it was a strange choice, but Alexander chose to stand in the spot facing the city and the sun while it was rising. This also meant it would be a lot easier for Aaron to see Alexander than it would be for Alexander to clearly see Aaron.

3 Both duels happened in Weehawken, New Jersey, in the same area. It was a popular spot for duels.

4 Aaron was good at aiming, and there were some unproven rumors that he had been practicing his shooting skills for three months before the duel. Alexander probably had not fired a gun since the war against Britain, more than 20 years before this duel.

5 Theodosia was Aaron's only child. At the time of this duel, she was 21 years old and married to a wealthy man. Alexander and Eliza had seven children at the time of the duel, from age two to 20.

6 The only people who were at the duel and survived to say what happened were William, Nathaniel, and

Aaron. (The doctor was waiting near the boat and did not see anything.) William said Alexander fired his gun first. Nathaniel said Aaron shot first, and Alexander's gun only went off because his body reacted out of his control when the bullet hit him. Aaron claimed he shot at Alexander a few seconds *after* Alexander's shot missed him.

So, what's true? All we know for sure is Alexander's bullet hit a tree branch far above Aaron's head and off to the side of where Aaron stood. No matter who shot first, we know Alexander did not aim at Aaron. And we know Aaron did aim right at Alexander.

7 John Laurens died when the war was ending, 22 years earlier, at age 27. George Washington had died just a few years before Alexander's duel with Aaron, from a sudden and mysterious illness, at age 67.

8 When Alexander was shot, he knew right away he was probably not going to live very much longer. He fell to the ground and instantly said, "I am a dead man." Nathaniel called for the doctor, who ran up the path to get to where the duel had happened.

Aaron walked toward Alexander, and Nathaniel said later that Aaron seemed to regret what had happened. But before Aaron could reach Alexander, William warned Aaron he couldn't allow the doctor to see his face. They had to leave quickly, before the doctor arrived. As the two of them ran to their boat, Aaron said to William, "I must go and speak to him." William again warned Aaron that was not a good idea. Instead, Aaron returned to the boat and William went back to check on Alexander so he could tell Aaron how he was doing.

-Adapted from Ron Chernow's biography, "Alexander Hamilton"

9 Alexander was actually taken to his friend's William Bayard, Jr.'s house. That is where the doctor took care of him and where he died the next afternoon.

10 Aaron went into hiding in Philadelphia for a little while after the duel, because he thought he might be arrested for murder.

46. WHO LIVES, WHO DIES, WHO TELLS YOUR STORY

Eliza shares what she hopes Alexander's legacy will be

Alexander is gone, and many people from his life share what they think about his **legacy**—the difference he made in the world and how people will remember him.

George Washington had died a few years before Alexander, but his spirit returns to remind everyone that no one has any control over who lives or who dies, or how the story of your life is told after you are gone. It's the people who live after you who decide what people will know about you and how they will remember you.

Thomas admits that even though he never liked Alexander, his plan for the country's money was really, really smart, and no other plan would have been better. James admits Alexander helped save the United States by fixing the debt problems after the war. His plan made it possible for the country to grow and continue to get better and better.

Angelica says all the other important people who helped create the country—the "**founding fathers**"—were able to live long lives and are talked about over and over again throughout history. She wants Alexander to be remembered for what he did, the same way they are. Who will make sure people remember him? Who will make sure his legacy lasts long after he is gone?

Eliza.

Eliza decides she wants to help tell Alexander's story after all. She lives **FIFTY** more years after Alexander dies—all the way to age 97. She is grateful for the extra time she gets to live. She works hard every day to keep Alexander's legacy going and to make a difference in the world herself. [1]

Eliza interviews soldiers who fought in battles with Alexander, to learn everything she can about his experience in the war. She organizes and reads through Alexander's many, many writings,[2] to keep them safe and to help tell the story of who he was and the things he did. Angelica helps Eliza with this project, since she loved Alexander, too, and because it is so important to her sister.[3]

Eliza raises money for a monument in Washington, D.C. to help everyone remember George Washington. She speaks up about how wrong slavery is. She believes Alexander would have done a lot more to try and end slavery if he hadn't been so busy with everything else and if he had lived longer.[4] She wonders, will she be able to do enough to help people remember and honor Alexander? Will people in the future remember the story of their life together and their love?

Eliza has done so much, but she is most proud of creating the first **orphanage** in New York City, which is a home for children who have lost their parents. When she looks into the children's eyes, she imagines seeing Alexander as a child, and it makes her heart so happy to be helping them. She knows giving these kids a chance to grow up and do great things is one of her greatest legacies.[5]

Eliza hopes people will always remember Alexander the way she wants them to, and she hopes she has done enough to make an important difference for as many children as possible. She can't wait to see Alexander again, someday, when her time on earth ends and she goes to heaven.[6]

Who will tell your story? What will they say about you? How will you be remembered?

---

1 It was really important to Eliza to be able to tell Alexander's story, especially because after he died his political enemies said and wrote some not very nice things about him. Because Alexander wasn't alive to defend himself, Eliza wanted to make sure the world knew the kind of person she believed he was and the many great things he did for the country.

-Adapted from Ron Chernow's biography, "Alexander Hamilton" (Prologue, p.2)

2 Altogether, there are now 22,000 pages of Alexander's writings that have been collected. That's more than 100 copies of this book added together—but with a lot more words on each page!

3 Eliza also paid about 30 people to help her go through Alexander's papers. But it was her son, John, who helped the most by spending several years writing and publishing his father's **biography**, which is the story about his life.

4 A note from the author: We all make choices about how we want to spend our time and what matters most to us. John Laurens devoted his work to ending slavery, and Alexander definitely could have done more if it was important to him.

5 The orphanage Eliza helped create still exists today! It is now called Graham Windham and helps 5,000 children and families each year.

6 Eliza was a Christian and strongly believed she would see Alexander again in heaven when she died. One night, when she was very old, she said "I am so tired. It is so long. I want to see Hamilton."

glossary

The definitions below explain the word the way it is used in the story. Words with a * are explained in more detail in the sidebars, or gray boxes, in the story.

accommodation: a compromise

affair: not being faithful to one's husband or wife

aim: ability to hit or shoot a specific spot

ambition: a person's desire to do great things

amendment: a change, such as to the Constitution

anonymous: the author's name is not listed

ballot: voting sheet

battle: a big fight, especially in a military war

biography: a story about someone's life

blow people away: amaze them

bolder: being even braver and doing bigger things

Cabinet: a group of people the president choses to help him or her run the country; each person is in charge of a different area of government

capital: the city where most people in the country's government work

colonist: a person who lives in a colony (see **colony**)

*colony: a group of people who live in a new place than the country they are originally from, but who are still considered to be part of their original country. The new land where they live is also called a colony.

command: a group of soldiers someone is in charge of

compromise: a deal or agreement

*****Congress**: part of the united States government. The people in each state vote to choose who they want to be in Congress to represent them. Members of Congress have discussions, and they create and vote on laws for the country.

Constitution: a set of rules for a country

Continental Army: the Colonial Army, or American Army

dawn: before the sun comes up

dearest: the most special

debt: money owed

demands satisfaction: asks for an apology

despair: having absolutely no hope

devastated: very heartbroken and incredibly sad

dowry: a wedding gift a woman's family gave to her husband to thank him for marrying her, and as a way for her to contribute financially to the marriage

*****duel**: a planned fight, with weapons, between two people, used as a way to defend an insulted person's reputation or honor

economy: how a country's money works

ensemble: group of people on stage in a performance

*****enslaved people**: people who were captured and then sold or traded to other people for goods, like food, cloth, drinks, and weapons. They were separated from their family and friends. Most of the enslaved people in the American Colonies were taken from the continent of Africa.

enslaver: someone who forced people to work for free

evidence: proof

faint: when a person's brain suddenly goes to sleep

federal government: government for the whole country, as one big group, sometimes called "central government." Makes decisions or laws that affect everyone in the country.

flirt: to say funny, sweet, or romantic things to a person to try to get them to like you

founding father: one of just a few people who are remembered in United States history for doing the most work to create, or found, the country.

governor: the leader of a state

grace: kindness and forgiveness

historian: someone who studies history

*House of Representatives: the part of Congress where each state gets a certain number of people to represent it depending on how many people live in that state. States with a lot of people have more representatives than states that don't have as many people.

hurricane: a very powerful storm with lots of wind and rain

impartial: not taking sides

*legacy: what people remember about you after you are gone

Lieutenant Colonel: someone in charge of soldiers. There are many levels of military officers, including Colonel, Major General, General, and more.

Loyalist: someone who lives in the American Colonies and is loyal to the King and Great Britain

make a name for oneself: do something to try to become famous or remembered

metaphor: when one thing is called something else that feels, acts, looks, or seems similar to it

negotiation: a discussion where the people involved are trying to come to an agreement

neutral: not helping either side in an argument

opponents: people on opposite sides

orphan: a child who no longer has a parent

orphanage: a home for children who do not have parents

Patriot: someone who lives in the American Colonies and supports or fights for freedom from Britain

published: or printed

refute: argue against something, try to prove it wrong

reputation: what other people think of a person

resign: to quit one's job

retreat: turn away and leave

*revolution: a war—a really big fight—where people want a big change in their government; such as when the American Colonies wanted to be their own country instead of having the King be in charge of them

rewind: go back; turn back time to replay something that happened

rich: having a lot of money

right-hand man: a close friend or trusted partner

rise up: go higher; to rise up in life means to gain a higher social status

rumors: stories people hear and share that might or might not be true

run for office: when someone wants to try to get elected, or have people vote for them

sarcastic: a way of joking when a person says something he or she does not mean

satisfied: happy

second: a friend who helps someone in a duel

*Senate: the part of Congress where the same number of people represent each state (two). These representatives are called Senators.

shot: a chance or opportunity

*slave: (see the definition of **enslaved people**)

*social class and social status: a way to divide people into groups and give them a label based on how much money, education, or land they have, or what kind of job they have

tailor: someone who makes and fixes clothes to fit individual customers

taxes: extra money people pay to the government that goes toward helping everyone

term: a set period of time; a president's term in office is four years

title: job name

toast: when someone stands up and says nice things about someone in front of everyone else

training: practice

treaty: deal or agreement

troops: a group of soldiers; or, when used with a number (like "32,000 troops"), it means that many soldiers

will: an important document that tells people where a person wants his or her money and belongings to go when he or she is no longer alive

yield: to let the other person win; in a duel, it means to admit the other person has won and to end the duel

---

further reading to explore

To learn more about Alexander Hamilton or the musical, talk to a grown-up about taking a look at these books and websites below. You can also check out some of the great kids' books about Alexander Hamilton or the American Revolution.

Grown-up Books

Hamilton: The Revolution, by Lin Manuel Miranda and Jeremy McCarter. Grand Central Publishing, 2016.
An in-depth look at the creation of the show, this also includes beautiful photographs, the lyrics to every song in the show, along with over 200 footnotes from Lin Manuel Miranda on the songs.

Alexander Hamilton, by Ron Chernow. Penguin Books, 2005.
The biography that inspired the musical, this gives so much rich detail to Alexander Hamilton's life, from his childhood on Nevis Island to his rising up in the American Colonies to become one of its "founding fathers."

Websites *(be sure to ask permission from a grown-up)*

Founders Online. https://founders.archives.gov/
This incredible site has more than 185,000 historical documents written by or to the "founding fathers": George Washington, Benjamin Franklin, John Adams, Thomas Jefferson, Alexander Hamilton, John Jay, and James Madison. You can read Alexander's letters to Eliza, his arguments with Thomas Jefferson, and much, much more.

Genius. https://genius.com/albums/Lin-manuel-miranda/Hamilton-an-american-musical-original-broadway-cast-recording
This site has notes from hundreds of visitors, including Lin Manuel Miranda, about almost *every* lyric in the show! Comments are about the meaning of the lyrics, the historical facts behind the events in the lyrics, the on-stage performance, the actors who starred in the opening cast on Broadway, and much more.

Personal Hamilton Research Collection.
https://www.pinterest.com/ajbh99/hamilton/
This is a collection of *most* of the research the author conducted to create this book, in addition to seeing the show, listening to the songs many, many times, and reading Ron Chernow's *Alexander Hamilton* and Lin Manuel Miranda's *Hamilton: The Revolution*. If you want one place to find lots of great information about the history *and* the musical, this is a great place to start.

acknowledgments

My most heartfelt thanks go out to every single friend, family member, and stranger on the internet who cheered me on throughout the journey of creating this book. A very special thanks to Amy L., the first friend I told about the idea for this book, for enthusiastically encouraging me to follow it through to reality.

Many thanks to my book launch team, who helped immensely by sharing their love for the book, to Amy D. for your incredible copyediting notes, to Abby and Kelley for your thoughtful feedback, and to everyone who sent me notes and suggestions along the way. And a huge thank you to Erin for taking the illustrations and turning them into an incredible cover design that is even more than I imagined it would be.

This book would not exist without the incredible, unmatched work of genius created by Lin-Manuel Miranda, *Hamilton: An American Musical*, inspired by Ron Chernow's riveting biography *Alexander Hamilton.* I have such deep gratitude for these two talented gentlemen and their collaborators. Without their dedication, time, sweat, tears, and perseverance, I—and the world—may never have discovered what a passionate, hard-working, driven person Alexander Hamilton was. I thank them for sharing his story through their writing, research, and talents.

To my mom, my lifelong cheerleader, for your shared

excitement and support throughout this entire process, thank you. And to Scott, who has generously supported this dream of mine by taking on much more than his share of parenting duties when I was writing and researching, for his time, patience, help with the eBook, and thoughts along the way: thank you, thank you, thank you. Having you both in my corner means the world to me.

And to Isabella, who selflessly offered to create the illustrations for this book, thank you for being such a wonderful partner. I never cease to be amazed by the amazing, talented, thoughtful, and beautiful person you are.

---

about the author

AMANDA BJERKAN HENNESSY grew up in the Midwest and has had a passion for writing since she was a child. *A Kids' Guide to Hamilton* was inspired by her adoration of the Broadway musical, along with her kids' love of the music and the many, many questions they had about it. Amanda has a B.A. in English and a B.A. & M.A. in Communication from the University of Illinois. She currently lives in sunny central Florida with her husband, Scott, and their two children, Giselle and Nathan. **Favorite song: "Wait For It"**

about the illustrator

ISABELLA BJERKAN is a high school student who lives in the Chicago suburbs and loves her Cairn Terrier, Chewbacca, and her family. She loves to play soccer and tennis, and she has had the opportunity to travel to Europe twice for tournaments. When she's not practicing, playing, or doing schoolwork, Isabella enjoys drawing, creating her own stickers, making music, and watching Netflix. **Favorite songs: "Burn," "The Story of Tonight"**

A final note:

If you enjoyed this book, please ask a grown-up to leave a review on Amazon. Reviews are super helpful for independent authors (like me) and help other people learn more about the book.

Thank you!